The Higher
Spiritual Path

The Higher Spiritual Path

William Wilson Quinn

BOOKS

Winchester, UK
Washington, USA

JOHN HUNT PUBLISHING

First published by O-Books, 2023
O-Books is an imprint of John Hunt Publishing Ltd., 3 East St., Alresford,
Hampshire SO24 9EE, UK
office@jhpbooks.com
www.johnhuntpublishing.com
www.o-books.com

For distributor details and how to order please visit the 'Ordering' section on our website.

ISBN: 978 1 80341 259 7
978 1 80341 260 3 (ebook)
Library of Congress Control Number: 2022942146

A CIP catalogue record for this book is available from the British Library.

Design: Lapiz Digital Services

UK: Printed and bound by CPI Group (UK) Ltd, Croydon, CR0 4YY
Printed in North America by CPI GPS partners

The author of this book does not dispense medical advice or
prescribe the use of any technique as a form of treatment for
physical, emotional, or medical problems without the advice of a
physician, either directly or indirectly. The intent of the author
is only to offer information of a general nature to help you in
your quest for emotional and spiritual well-being. In the event
you use any of the information in this book for yourself, which is
your constitutional right, the author and the publisher assume no
responsibility for your actions.

We operate a distinctive and ethical publishing philosophy in
all areas of our business, from our global network of authors to
production and worldwide distribution.

Other Titles by this Author

The Only Tradition
ISBN: 0-7914-3213-0

Articles of Aquarius
ISBN: 978-1-931942-82-9

The Chela's Handbook
ISBN: 978-1-61852-128-6

Dedicated to the Few

Acknowledgments

Foremost among those responsible for the existence of this book is my colleague, friend, and fellow traveler Idarmis Rodriguez, whose much appreciated insights and skills are reflected throughout its pages. In addition, I wish to thank Frank Smecker, editor *par excellence*, Elizabeth Radley, and Gavin Davies of John Hunt Publishing for their assistance and professionalism in bringing this book to fruition. Finally, gratitude is a word insufficient to express my true feeling for the unremitting support and encouragement of my partner, Louise, not only with regard to my labors on this book, but for everything else I undertook during this past decade with her, and may yet undertake.

Contents

Introduction

Upon first scanning the title of this work, some readers may ask themselves what the author means by "higher spiritual path." Because this term and the related term "wayfarer" are used so frequently throughout, it seems only fair to orient the reader at the outset with regard to these terms, as much rests upon their proper understanding. First, in this work the word "wayfarer," often used to identify those on a spiritual quest, simply refers to a man or woman who is treading the "higher spiritual path." That being said, the onus of definition is then transferred to the precise meaning of the term "higher spiritual path." By this term we mean a rigorous and invariably difficult path of spiritual development and training whose initial objective is becoming an accepted *chela*—a Sanskrit term meaning pupil or disciple—of a *guru*.

However, we do not refer here to ordinary *gurus* or spiritual teachers who now populate the transient world. Rather, we refer to those of both East and West who as Adepts have achieved the very highest levels of advancement in the knowledge and applications of the *philosophia perennis* or perennial philosophy, also known by other names and terms like *theosophia* and *ātma-vidyā*. Thus, while there are many whose spiritual practices may extend no further than reading spiritually oriented literature or practicing meditation and various dietary and yogic disciplines in the course of otherwise worldly lives, such individuals would not be defined here as treading the *higher* spiritual path.

But for wayfarers who do tread the higher spiritual path, including such activities as those just mentioned, this path *becomes* their lives almost exclusively. They are those who recognize the truth of the fact that the principal questions and issues—and even meaning—of life are not political, or social, or economic, or religious, but *spiritual*. Their solitary focus becomes the objective of not only chelaship, but ultimately of initiation into that sacred and eternal yet reclusive Order of Adepts who are their *gurus*. While these wayfarers may, as *chelas*, yet be "in" the world, spiritually they are no longer "of" it. Greater detail pertaining to both this higher spiritual path, and the Adepts who guide the wayfarers upon it, await those who choose to read further into these pages.

The pivotal Sanskrit terms *nirvāna* and *moksha* are defined, or have otherwise been written about, in various ways. Yet most of their definitions, or descriptions, can only be approximations of the sublime reality conveyed by these terms. This is because both refer to a metaphysical state of being, common to the discourse of traditional Buddhism and Hinduism respectively, which is transcendental and unconditional, and so cannot accurately be circumscribed by language, or even by thought. It is effectively a state of eternal bliss (*ānanda*) that may only be entered by the spiritual wayfarer or initiate when, after numerous incarnations whose last few have included treading the higher spiritual path, he or she is liberated: released forever on this physical plane from the wheel of death and rebirth and all its attendant suffering.

Unique to the Buddhist religion is a traditional and scripturally based difference of perspectives arising from an ultimate *choice* that confronts the spiritually advanced person who has achieved what in Pāli is known as *vimutti*. This word is typically defined as "deliverance" or "release," and refers narrowly to the event of liberation from the wheel of death and rebirth. This choice that promptly follows *vimutti*, then, is whether such a liberated being should choose immediate entry into *nirvāna*, or choose to defer it. This choice is based upon the question of whether it is preferable (i) to proceed into the bliss of *nirvāna*, evermore beyond the pale of suffering in a bodily or physical existence, or (ii) to intentionally and voluntarily defer—

in fact, *sacrifice*—immediate reintegration into that blissful state of oneness in order to serve others. In contrast to choosing the bliss of *nirvāna*, the choice or sacrifice of its deferment entails remaining incarnate in a bodily or physical existence (or at least in a state that is not *nirvāna*) and continuing to suffer the vicissitudes of *samsāra* (the transient world of illusion and suffering) in order to help other human beings achieve *vimutti*, or liberation.

Moreover, the vast duration of this sacrifice extends to the point in human spiritual evolution where ultimately *all* human beings have at last achieved liberation. Only then may he or she who has elected to make this sacrifice—who has elected to follow the path of the *bodhisattva*—finally enter the nirvanic state having fulfilled this sacred promise to help all other sentient beings achieve that goal.

The former path of immediate entrance into *nirvāna* upon one's liberation is described in Buddhist terms as that of the *pratyeka* Buddha. The latter path of voluntarily deferring this blissful reward in order to alleviate the suffering of others and help them to achieve liberation, is described in Buddhist terms as that of the *bodhisattva*. These two paths are significantly different, and the choice of either path points to the basic nature and character of each spiritual aspirant who chooses. That of the *pratyeka* Buddha who immediately enters *nirvāna* indicates a resolute and diligent adherent of the *dharma* and practitioner of all those virtues set forth in the Buddhist "eightfold path," being the last of the Four Noble Truths of the Buddha, without any need for further spiritual or occult training.

The choice of the path of the *bodhisattva* coexists with the ascent of the wayfarer or initiate on the higher spiritual path, and together these indicate a sacrificial and compassionate nature. This path requires extraordinary strength and courage, and a willingness to undergo rigorous training in mastering the forces of Nature both prior to achieving *vimutti*, and even after. Such training is a requirement in order for new initiates to operate more effectively and efficiently in order to succeed in bringing more light to the "great orphan," or humanity, during the long remainder of their existences in the physical realm, even while having been liberated from it. It is important to note here that while we may have been using Buddhist terms and textual references so far in our discussion, this profound subject in actual fact describes a *universal* choice among all advanced spiritual seekers and esotericists worldwide, Buddhist or otherwise, who have advanced to that point in their long spiritual journeys. It is because Buddhist terms to describe this choice are convenient— because they already exist—that they are used here. But we cannot emphasize strongly enough that this choice, and these paths, are universal and therefore applicable to *all* those who tread the higher spiritual path regardless of religion, ethnicity or race.

True spiritual journeys follow a pattern. From time immemorial, at their beginning stages the paths of those genuinely seeking higher spiritual truth are multiple and varied. The journeys of spiritual seekers undertaken at the beginning stage have typically traversed and still traverse the entire spectrum of the world's religions and sacred societies. These journeys may often, as the wayfarer advances, include participation in active and esoterically oriented hieratic communities, such as ashrams or monasteries, under the tutelage of a resident teacher. Yet at some point in this pattern, whether years or lifetimes in duration from this journey's outset, depending upon the character and purity of the individual wayfarer the opportunity to advance even farther along the spiritual path may present itself.

At this juncture, the multiple and varied spiritual paths begin to fuse and to become singular and invariable. It is as if, at the very beginning, these diverse spiritual paths are all at the base of a grand pyramid. And for those wayfarers who voluntarily and purposefully ascend the steep pyramid of spiritual truth to its higher reaches toward the narrowing apex, these formerly outer paths become inner or metaphysical ones, which necessarily draw closer together and eventually merge to become effectively *one* higher spiritual path. Finally, through the sacred rite of initiation, those on all spiritual paths who qualify are led to that *single* path whose invariable destination is the topmost point of the pyramid's apex. Once upon this highest path—that of the *bodhisattva*—the initiate thereafter treads solely for the benefit of humanity, sacrificing his or her own release from the wheel of death and rebirth until the entirety of humanity gains its final liberation.

Those seekers of higher spiritual truth, those wayfarers, who succeed in making this climb from the base of the metaphoric spiritual pyramid to its apex will there encounter special teachers—*gurus*—who, like themselves, also succeeded in ascending the summit of this difficult, momentous climb. These elect teachers are able to instruct the newly successful wayfarers in the more esoteric and extensive truths or realities of the universe, of *nature* in its totality, that may not have been accessible to their former religious or spiritual teachers who guided them at the outset of their sacred journeys. These venerable teachers, found at this apex, form a brother/sister-hood of Adepts comprised of a diverse and extraordinarily select group of men and women that one would not ordinarily find in any orthodox religious community. Collectively, these Adepts form a *spiritual* hierarchy of humanity, having achieved highly advanced levels of spiritual awareness and consciousness and capability through lifetimes of study, training, ordeal, and sacrifice. The non-denominational and eternal spiritual truths and principles taught by these Adepts are those of what in Latin is termed the *philosophia perennis*.

Access to interaction with and ultimately discipleship of these Adepts is not easy. This is so because the key to this access lies solely in the hands of the aspiring wayfarer, who *alone* must achieve an exceptional level of purification and be endowed with an indefeasible strength and determination in order to gain this access. When the resolute wayfarer ascending the pyramid's apex has become spiritually pure and thoroughly selfless, and commands enough courage and strength, the way will open. This milestone is normally marked by the wayfarer formally becoming an accepted *chela*, and so beginning a personal *chela-guru* relationship with one of the Adepts. But up to that life-changing point, one such Adept wrote, consistent with their extreme reclusivity, that "We rarely show any outward signs by which to be recognized or sensed." Fortunately for those for whom this goal has not been realized, but for whom it may be proximate, there exists considerable guidance and instruction on how interaction with these Adepts may be commenced—and maintained—by treading the higher spiritual path.

What follows in the essays of this work is designed to help clarify this guidance and instruction the Adepts have given us through their own writings and those of their advanced *chelas*. The subjects of the essays, when viewed together as a whole, are meant to cover as much of the multiple principles and doctrines, in addition to the tasks, ordeals and challenges of ascending the higher spiritual path as the author could devise. No claim, however, is being made that these specific subjects and their treatment are comprehensive—far from it. So, it is up to each wayfarer to complete the inquiry, and discover for himself or herself what else may be needed to reach the summit that marks the height of the ascent of the higher spiritual path.

1

Mountain and Summit as the Path and Its Goal

In point of fact, there is nowhere in physical nature a mountain abyss so hopelessly impassable and obstructive to the traveler as that spiritual one, which keeps them back from me.

– Morya

The motion picture *Everest*, released in 2015, is a large-screen adventure drama about skilled mountaineers who attempted to scale the summit of Mount Everest, which received deserved critical acclaim. Featuring international film stars, the film is based on a true story and depicts real events of the Mount Everest disaster in May of 1996. The story focuses on attempts of two separate expedition groups of climbers to survive a deadly high-altitude blizzard. Multiple climbers were on the mountain near the summit when the blizzard hit unexpectedly, its gale force winds driving snow and ice against the climbers like explosive debris. Eight climbers caught in the blizzard died on Mount Everest during that tragic event. Up to that point in time, it was the single deadliest day on Mount Everest.

But that lamentable single-day record in 1996 was subsequently broken by the deaths of sixteen climbers (Sherpa guides) resulting from the 2014 Mount Everest ice avalanche. Thereafter, the 2014 record was again broken by the fatalities of twenty-two climbers on the mountain resulting from multiple avalanches caused by the massive 2015 earthquake in Nepal.

Films—and books—relating such stories point to the fact that there is, and always has been, a fascination in the collective psyche of humankind that pertains to the difficulty and risks associated with the ascent of a high-altitude mountain summit, and the rewards that accrue to the successful climber. This natural relationship between (i) mountain/summit and (ii) ascent also supports the use of simile in which arduous challenge in the ascent of a mountain summit is likened to other challenging human endeavors. Stated alternatively, this relationship can be made comparable to a variety of other human endeavors by virtue of its stark clarity and its simple comprehensibility. Not the least of those human endeavors is treading the higher spiritual path over all or a portion of one's lifetime, and the difficulty of reaching its sacred summit, being the apex of spiritual truth. One can, in fact, make a persuasive argument that the difficulty and arduousness of a person achieving the summit of life's spiritual ascent actually *exceed* those of ascending to the summit of Mount Everest, and so requires an even greater degree of courage, discipline, fitness, and steadfastness.

For everyone including the seasoned mountaineer, the climb to a mountain's summit is exhausting, difficult, and often dangerous, as witnessed just by the multiple deaths on Mount Everest since 1996. The laws of gravity explain why it is more exhausting than walking along a path on flat or gradual terrain. Sheer cliffs, powerful winds, and icy, rugged topography and altitude, all depending on the mountain in question, explain why it is similarly more difficult and dangerous. These indisputable facts are no doubt the genesis for repeated use of the mountain, and its summit, as apt similes and metaphors for the challenge of a person's higher spiritual journey, particularly where the purpose and goal of that spiritual journey are fully understood by the traveler.

Once the summit is finally reached, the climber experiences a clear and panoramic vision of all around, and all below, together with a greater proximity to and unobstructed view of all the heavenly bodies beyond the Earth's curtilage. It is therefore not hard to understand how this achievement of reaching the summit may be correlated either to the clarity inherent in the experience of taking a regular initiation as a *chela* of an Adept or, as significantly, having become what in Sanskrit is referred to as a *jivanmukta*—one who, while yet incarnate, has at last liberated himself or herself from the wheel of death and rebirth—and from the bonds of lower or mundane earthly life. But one does not achieve this summit without first climbing the forbidding mountain.

The use of both metaphor and simile in correlating the ascent of mountain and summit to one's higher spiritual journey follows a long tradition by writers of theosophic and esoteric treatises. This is closely related to the fact that the phenomena of mountain and summit—including their ascent—occur regularly, and with elaborate detail in some cases, in the world's great and immemorial cosmogonic and cosmological myths. Though these myths differ in specifics, the representations of mountain and summit in them tend to share certain traits in common, such as the summits of the mountains being the "home of the gods" or, as often, the divine intersection between heaven and earth. The experience of Moses ascending the jagged summit of Mount Sinai, for example, and there witnessing an awesome theophany, resulted in the revelation of the Ten Commandments as a moral and spiritual guide for the entirety of humankind. Motifs of mountain and summit appearing in many of the world's cosmogonic myths are, moreover, often inextricably related to the difficulties of the climb, of ascending those summits.

All ancient or traditional mythology is deemed sacred within the cultures it informs. This is especially true of those myths that can be categorized as cosmogonic and which describe the creation and placement of the universe, the firmament, and our world, with all its constituent localities. This is important to note because where mountains and summits appear prominently in such myths, they are typically imbued with the *sacred* which, as will be seen, corresponds perfectly to the use of mountain-summit metaphors in life's spiritual journey. Two of many other

9

possible examples from traditional mythology follow here, in order to illustrate this point.

In classical Hindu mythology, various differences occur in the story of creation depending upon whether one looks to the oral *sruti* tradition of Vedic ritual and doctrine or the oral *smrti* tradition emphasizing the acts of gods and kings, both later transcribed and in large part comprising the *purānas*. Nonetheless, after the world was formed, one aspect of it looms large in Indic myths, which is the placement and location of Mount Meru, commonly believed to be the abode of Brahma. In the myths Meru is a mountain in the far north—in relation to the Indian subcontinent—which is sacred not only to Hindus, but to Jains and some Buddhists as well. Helena P. Blavatsky (hereafter and throughout this work "HPB") refers to its mythological status as "the abode of the gods."[1] Mount Meru, pursuant to its mythological reality, is considered to be the center of all the physical *and* metaphysical universes, and so has a primordial spiritual dimension. In testimony to this, Hindu, Jain, and Buddhist temples have been constructed in past centuries as symbolic representations of Mount Meru.

According to the great Hindu epic *Mahābhārata*—which we should also note contains within it the *Bhagavad Gita*—the five sons of King Pandu, known as the Pandavas, and their wife Draupadi, attempted to ascend to the summit of Mount Meru in order to attain heaven. But during the ascent Draupadi and four of the brothers fell to their deaths due to their sinful karma. Only the fifth brother, Yudhisthira, because of his spiritual purity, successfully climbed to the mountain's summit and so reached the sacred sanctuary of heaven. Such traditional myths encapsulate beautifully both the notions of mountain/summit as sacred space, and the risks and difficulty of attaining that space posed by attempting to ascend to this sacred summit.

This Eastern example of Mount Meru corresponds in many ways to the Western example of Mount Olympus, the dwelling place of Zeus, chief of the Greek gods. In Greek mythology Mount Olympus was home to the twelve Olympian gods who, including Zeus, ruled the ancient Greek world. Olympus' northern slope was, further, the birthplace of the nine Muses and home to several of them. Mount Olympus is the location in which many Greek myths are set, and from whose "topmost peak," as described by Homer in the *Iliad*, Zeus commands the other gods. Unlike Mount Meru, Olympus has an actual geographical counterpart, which is Greece's highest mountain in Thessaly. But like Mount Meru, Olympus is imbued with the same consecrating power of height, of proximity to and participation in the sacred, and also shares the same spatial symbolism of transcendence that includes, among other things, the principle of the vertical axis as contained in the ancient notion of the *axis mundi*. Unlike Mount Meru, entry to Olympus was prohibited to mortals, who were not permitted within the confines of its sacred summit. However, any mortal who in defiance of that rule nonetheless succeeded in accessing those sacred peaks of Olympus became—just like those who ascended Mount Meru—spiritually consecrated and usually achieved the status of gods, or demi-gods. According to the exploits of the Dioscouri, or the twin half-brothers Castor and Pollux, such was the outcome for Castor, the mortal twin.

In summary, the world's great sacred cosmogonic myths that feature icons of mountain and summit as representations of the principles of *center*, and *transcendence*, and *vertical* or *spiritual hierarchy*, are the immemorial bases for use by later writers of the metaphor that equates ascent of these summits to the challenges of a person's spiritual journey in life. And, even more particularly do we find this equation applied to the daunting sacrifices of the wayfarer's ascent of the higher spiritual path. Just what these challenges and sacrifices are, and their degrees of difficulty—and of suffering—will be our focus throughout this work.

Before returning our full attention to the core of this essay, we first urge the reader to remember a common though important terminological usage in the discourse of the spiritual journey. This common usage will provide more clarity in further examining the metaphor of climbing a mountain summit for climbing to the summit of truth, of spiritual realization, in one's spiritual journey through this incarnation. It is the terminology or usage of, and distinction between, the "Inner" Person and the "Outer" Person, which principle may alternately be referred to as one's Higher Self and Lower Self. These and synonymous terms have been used throughout time to express this concept in sacred scriptures and commentary, and it found perhaps its best—or at least most succinct—expression in the West by Thomas Aquinas, who noted that *"duo sunt in homine"*[2] ("two there are in man"). Aquinas' term reflects equally not only a core Platonic doctrine but the Buddhist and Hindu doctrines of the two selves, mortal and immortal, that dwell together in one person.

This doctrine of the two selves relies upon, and can only be fully explained by, the corpus of complex esoteric teachings that deal with the *seven human principles* derived largely from the pertinent Sanskrit terms of *śarīras* and *kośas* found in the principal Upanishads, and often translated as "vehicles" or "sheaths" or "bodies." For ease of understanding, the lower four of these seven principles are said to comprise the "lower quaternary," and the higher three the "higher triad." Those familiar with this septenary system of human principles further understand that the lower quaternary is often referred to as the Outer Person or Lower Self, while the higher triad is similarly referred to as the Inner Person or Higher Self. This useful bifurcation is a further reduction of the complex reality of these seven principles divided into these two portions of a person, and more detailed treatment of this reality will follow throughout. For now, it will suffice to understand that the final dualistic reduction to

Inner and Outer Person is even more efficient a tool to utilize in discussing the broader issues of spiritual development where these multiple principles or vehicles are not the specific topic of discussion. It should be noted here that HPB used exactly these terms—Inner and Outer Person—not infrequently in her writings for that reason.

In addition to the usage of the terms "Inner" and "Outer" Person, the reader is also asked to keep in mind the choice confronted in traditional Buddhist doctrine between the way of the *bodhisattva* and the way of the *pratyeka* Buddha. To repeat, this choice faces those who finally achieve *vimutti* or "release" from the wheel of death and rebirth and its component illusions (*samsara*), and amounts to either (i) deferring entrance into *nirvāna* for the sake of others, or (ii) immediate entrance into *nirvāna*. Since this topic was discussed in the Introduction above, we add here only the further point that some commentators ascribe these differing emphases, respectively, as endemic to the Mahāyāna (including Vajrayāna) and the Theravāda schools or divisions of Buddhism. But this ascription is neither entirely accurate nor absolute.

We return now to the central question at issue here, which is how and to what extent the metaphor of ascending the summit of an actual mountain correlates to the ascent of the summit of spiritual truth and the rigorous higher path that must be tread to achieve this. How, we may also ask, does this metaphor relate specifically to the daily lives of those on this higher spiritual journey? A good place to begin to find an answer to these questions is to reproduce a quote from Annie Besant, in which she employs this metaphor in a unique way by identifying two separate ways to achieve the summit. She writes:

The man who has entered on the probationary [spiritual] path intends to accomplish within a very limited number of lives what the man of the world will accomplish in hundreds upon hundreds of lives. He is like the man who, wanting to reach the top of the mountain, refuses to follow the track that winds round and round. He says: 'I am going straight up the mountain-side, I am not going to waste my time on this winding beaten track which will take me so long, the slow way on which most of the going is smooth and easy, beaten by the myriads of feet that tread it. I shall go by the shorter route, I shall take the swifter path, I shall go straight up the mountain-side. No matter what the difficulties, I will climb the mountain. No matter what obstacles there may be, I will go; precipices there may be—I will cross them; walls of rocks there may be—I will climb them; obstacles and boulders in my path there may be—I will manage in some way to surmount them or get round them; but up that mountain-side I mean to travel.' What will be the result? He will find a thousand-fold more difficulties surround him on the path. If he gains in time he must pay in trouble for the difficulty of the achievement. The man who enters on the probationary path is the man who chooses the short way to the mountain-top, and calls down on himself the whole of his past Karma, which is largely to be got rid of before he is fitted for initiation.[3]

In her version of the mountain summit and ascent metaphor, Besant draws an interesting and insightful distinction between two different approaches to the ascent of the summit. While one may be tempted here to draw a comparison or correlation between Besant's two approaches to ascending the summit and our prior distinction between the division in Buddhism that emphasizes the (i) ideal of the *bodhisattva* and the (ii) ideal of the *pratyeka* Buddha, the facts cannot support it. There are too many spiritually exalted Buddhist contemplatives in Theravāda "forest tradition" meditation centers and *sanghas* to allow such a correlation, and for this reason one should not infer that this is what Besant meant. Accordingly, in our version of this metaphor—which, when completed, may as easily be viewed as a parable—we will concentrate on those taking the path of the *bodhisattva*, *i.e.*, those who wish to go "straight up the mountainside" in Besant's words, regardless of their religious affiliations, their races, or their ethnicities.

Our focus on those who follow the way of the *bodhisattva* highlights the imminent and greater, or perhaps "compressed," rigors of those treading that shorter path to the summit, which is effectively the higher spiritual path. There exists an ancient and hierarchical structure comprised of those few who have similarly gone before on this shorter and more arduous path of the *bodhisattva* and achieved the summit of spiritual truth, and who then often become the teachers of those presently engaged in a direct climb to the summit. Because these wayfarers elect to work thereafter for humanity, they will need to learn and acquire through disciplined development certain latent capabilities and skills. After their initial acceptance to chelaship, and even after initiations, these climbers undergo considerable training in mastering the forces of Nature, among other things, throughout their journeys. In addition, as Besant suggests, these wayfarers, because of their voluntarily accelerated ascent to the summit of truth, must also undergo a correspondingly accelerated confrontation with their own karma, the result of which often involves great suffering and hardship during the initial period. Those who elect to climb straight up the mountain to the summit must forge their own paths, and the consequences of the many difficult decisions they make along this challenging way are theirs alone.

Those spiritual travelers—as metaphorical climbers—who make the choice to go straight up the mountain, to follow the *bodhisattva* ideal implicit in the higher spiritual path, are faced with burdens not faced by others. First, the climb straight up is far more difficult and exhausting than a gradual ascent, and thus requires an extraordinary degree of dedication and strength and determination, unlike that required of others. Second, the risk of injury or death on this steep climb is far greater than that faced by those taking the gradual ascent. In fact, considerable suffering compressed within a shorter time frame that occurs in the metaphoric form of injuries, if not death, is practically inescapable on the climb up this steep path. The law of compensation (*karma*) dictates this rule, because in this metaphor only those who have achieved a sufficient degree of spiritual purity, like the mythological Yudhisthira, can be successful in reaching the summit. And such spiritual purity occurs through resolution and a balancing of one's oppositive *karma*—equating to the Inner Person's victory by mastering the Outer Person following an agonizing struggle, *i.e.*, the direct climb of the higher spiritual path.

Tradition holds that there are no exceptions to this law. This is illustrated by the experience of Damodar Mavalankar of Bombay, who was one of HPB's and Henry S. Olcott's most cherished colleagues, and about whom few had anything to say but praise for his loyalty and dedication to these founders of The Theosophical Society and their mission. In early 1885 Damodar left India as an accepted *chela* bound for the Himalayan retreat of his teacher and *guru*, the Adept Koot Hoomi (hereafter and throughout this work "KH"). There was no word of Damodar's progress until a note from this Adept, transcribed on a letter, was received by Olcott in June of 1886. The note reads:

The poor boy [Damodar] has had his *fall*. Before he could stand in the presence of the 'Masters' he had to undergo the severest trials that a neophyte ever passed through, to atone for the many questionable things in which he had over-zealously taken part, bringing disgrace upon the sacred science and its adepts. The mental and physical suffering was too much for his weak frame, which has been quite prostrated, but he will recover in course of time. This ought to be a warning to you all. You have believed 'not wisely but too well.' To unlock the gates of the mystery you must not only lead a life of the strictest probity, but learn to discriminate truth from falsehood.[4]

From this we can learn how critical is the decision to begin a steep and direct ascent to the summit of truth, and why one should never fail to be fully aware of one's own character or to make uncritical assumptions about one's readiness to proceed. It is said in *John* 16:24, "ask, and ye shall receive," but this "asking" for chelaship—which may of itself be easy and which invariably prompts some response—should always be preceded by a sober and honest evaluation of one's readiness to "receive" and one's current circumstances. Figuratively speaking, failure to evaluate oneself honestly before asking to become a *chela* would be tantamount to setting out to climb the summit of Mount Everest without any physical training or necessary equipment—a decision with a probable outcome of tragedy.

But at the same time, one cannot allow excessive doubt or trepidation to preclude the decision to begin such an ascent. Unwavering courage is an absolute requirement for this ascent of the higher spiritual path. And always and repeatedly the Adepts communicating with principals of the theosophical movement of the late-nineteenth century exhorted them to *try*. This exhortation was often found in their correspondence in all upper-case letters: TRY.

Success in completing the difficult spiritual climb and ascending the summit of truth is, in a figurative sense, to suffer the defeat (*i.e.*, "death") of the Outer Person, which often fights with ferocity to avoid this outcome. Though the physical body may survive this death, the remainder of the Outer Person must be wholly reborn from one with personal wants and cravings and attachments, with emotional and mental desires and proclivities, to one whose motivations are completely unselfish and pure, and wholly subject to the directives of the Inner Person. There are fewer forms of "death" that elicit such a degree of suffering. The difficult *baseline* criteria for achieving this outcome are, among others, "Fasting, meditation, chastity of thought, word, and deed, silence for certain periods of time to enable nature herself to speak to him who comes to her for information; government of the animal passions and impulses; [and] utter unselfishness of intention..."[5] Following these requirements, suffering further the accelerated and heavy vicissitudes of karma visited upon the spiritual climber who decides to take the straight path up the mountain to the summit of truth is but another way to describe the process of this death of the Outer Person. This process typically occurs during the climb and must usually be completed before reaching the summit.

The spiritual climber, at the outset of his or her ascent of this seemingly indomitable mountain summit, should also be aware that there are no easy shortcuts to that summit. Extending the metaphor, one cannot ride an animal or a vehicle to the summit, or be carried in a palanquin, or take a helicopter. No amount of wealth or social or political influence can assist this climber in reaching the summit, nor can one take the place of another. Such a climber must use his or her *own* feet, and make the difficult climb himself or herself, alone. Along the way this climber will lose footing and at times slide painfully backwards, downhill. This climber will invariably suffer scrapes, and bruises, and broken bones, and frozen extremities, and debilitating fatigue. But despite such setbacks and injuries, the climber must nonetheless keep ascending if the goal is to be achieved. On the way up the higher spiritual path the climber's feet must eventually be "washed in the blood of the heart," flowing from a wound to the heart made by the piercing lance of sacrifice—sacrifice of the world of the self-absorbed Outer Person to that of the higher and nobler Inner Person. Such is an inescapable component of treading the higher spiritual path.

Certain aspirants may at last have come to a point in their long spiritual journeys where it is time to decide to undertake such an all-out ascent to the summit. At this early point they consider beginning to follow the way of the *bodhisattva*, and to actively invest the great effort that this choice entails with *complete* dedication. This choice is the decision to try. At first they may struggle mightily with the weight of this decision, as the consequences involved are usually formidable. For those climbers who live in the general population, the effects of this decision on their lives can be radical and may, as a first step, involve entrance or relocation into a monastery, ashram, or similar spiritual community.

In addition, for its very survival the Outer Person works forcefully *against* a decision to ascend the summit of truth. Even in our present time with global climate disasters, autocracy, aggression, disinformation and pandemics occurring at quicker intervals and spiritual darkness relentlessly pushing to envelop humanity, some aspirants may feel safer and more comfortable within the environments of their families and communities, and perhaps their employment. This places these aspirants at a disadvantage in facing the consequences of this personal decision. Standing on the very edge of this decision, some may even be ready without realizing it, but act instead through fear of uncertainty to preserve their familiar spiritual paths, and so avoid the uncomfortable results that flow from a *total* commitment to ascend directly the summit of truth.

Such a decision is never easy. It first requires an unblinking gaze into the depths of our hearts to discover whether we have the courage and the stamina to proceed. Once made, this decision can result in alterations to the various relationships we have, including those with our communities at large. Upon making our decision, our motives are sometimes misunderstood and criticized, ironically, as selfish or aloof. But it is said that "... he who cares for the opinion of the multitude will never soar above the crowd."[6] In some cases this decision may mean a sacrifice of these relationships, and certainly a sacrifice of our comfort and ease and sense of security. It usually means a handing over of what we believe is certainty in our life's path to uncertainty, and of a clearly planned direction to the unknown. For those spiritual climbers already resident in a spiritual community, this decision, even though free of some difficulties faced by those who are not residents of spiritual communities, is no less difficult. In short, it requires a surrender of the Outer to our Inner Person, which occurs through the simultaneous process of subduing and diminishing our reactive Outer Person, whose mundane wishes, habits, desires and attachments thereafter become unimportant.

The extraordinary difficulty of this decision to begin the direct ascent to the summit of truth—and upon succeeding devote oneself entirely to the enlightenment of the "orphan humanity"—is not new. In fact, it is ancient and has given rise to hoary maxims of truth about this higher spiritual journey like *multi vocati, electi pauci* ("many are called, few are chosen") which finds expression in Christian scripture in *Matthew* 22:14. And the fearsome danger in the direct climb to the summit is not new either, expressed by Besant as the climber calling "down on himself the whole of his past karma" by undertaking the way of the *bodhisattva*. This choice is immemorial, yet ever present.

Since the first ascent of Mount Everest's summit by Edmund Hillary in 1953, over 300 climbers to date have *died* trying to ascend that summit, and as many or more have been injured. But the direct climb to the summit of spiritual truth takes far longer, and is often as dangerous. The main difference between those who successfully ascend the summit of Mount Everest, and those who metaphorically ascend directly the summit of spiritual truth, is one of the greatest magnitude. Those who ascend to the summit of Mount Everest have arguably achieved the world's most magnificent vista, and have proven by a clear demonstration their attributes of supreme discipline and will. But those who succeed in ascending directly to the summit of spiritual truth, for all the woeful sacrifice and suffering of that rugged climb, have achieved something even more extraordinary as a consequence of their choice to serve humanity. One may believe, and not doubt, that arrival of these spiritual climbers at the summit signals their entry into a new world of wonder and magic, where they are immersed in a vast reservoir of unconditional *love*—a condition in which they and those with whom they labor for humanity remain as long as that service continues.

2

Purification and the Higher Spiritual Path

Serenity of mind, gentleness, silence, self-control,
purity of being are called the efforts of the mind.
– Bhagavad Gita (17.14-16)

It is of no use either to deny or to defend the fact that the Adepts and other high initiates of the ancient Order to which KH and his brother Morya belong are extraordinarily reclusive. Being so reclusive they are, accordingly, equally reticent to interact with the transient world and its inhabitants. It is therefore pointless to seek to deny or defend these attributes because their admitted and *self-described* reclusivity and reticence are undeniable and, moreover, are in no need of being defended. In line with these preferences, the Adept KH also declared that the "motto" of his Order is "To dare, to will, to act and remain silent."[1] It is pursuant to these aggregated facts of reclusivity, reticence, and silence that HPB, the "higher and initiated *chela*" of Morya, says of the initiates of this Order that "No true adept will on any consideration whatever reveal himself as one to the profane."[2]

While this Order does have strict or "adamantine" laws and rules, which the Adepts repeatedly emphasize in their writings, reclusivity and reticence are not *de jure* requirements among these rules. Rather, reclusivity and reticence are *de facto* necessities based on certain basic principles of "sacred science," which are neither judgmental nor biased. These principles often manifest as natural phenomena, such as sympathetic vibration. Moreover, we know through their writings that organizationally this ancient and venerable Order is hierarchical, and that the hierarchy of its initiate-members is based on criteria such as seniority, mastery of will force, degrees of initiation attained, and wisdom, among others. We also learn from their writings that the higher the initiate in this order, the greater the reclusivity and reticence he or she may need to adopt for interactions with the transient world. As KH tells us, "... the greater the powers of the Adept, the less he is in sympathy with the natures of the profane who often come to him saturated with the emanations of the outside world, those animal emanations of the selfish, brutal crowd that we so dread—the longer he was separated from that world... the purer he has himself become..."[3]

But though the Adepts are reluctant to enter the world of the "brutal crowd," they often allow their advanced *chelas* to "work in the world" on their behalf, as their agents, to further their primary mission of the enlightenment of humanity. In speaking about leaving their *chelas* to "fight their own battles" until they are qualified to serve as their agents working in the world, KH wrote that Adepts may have to show such restraint "... occasionally [even] with higher and *initiated* chelas such as H.P.B., once they are allowed to work in the world, that all of us more or less avoid."[4]

Such statements of "avoidance"—of reclusivity and reticence—appear in multiple places in the writings of these Adepts, and no attempts to hide or deny these self-described and clearly admitted preferences were ever made by them. "*Our ways are not your ways*," wrote KH to his *chela* Laura Holloway. "We rarely show any outward signs by which to be recognized or sensed."[5] Elsewhere he wrote to A.O. Hume, "Be it as it may, we are content to live as we do—unknown and undisturbed by a civilization which rests so exclusively upon intellect [*manas*]."[6]

Yet these discretionary preferences and behaviors of reclusivity and reticence by the Adepts and high initiates are neither arbitrary nor capricious. As was mentioned above, there are sound metaphysical or sacred-science reasons for them based on the Adepts' extraordinary levels of physical and psychic purification, brought about by advanced levels of spiritual development. In addition to sympathetic vibration and the law of correspondence, these sacred-scientific reasons also have to do with efficiency of the expenditure of their spiritual energy, with working within an unpolluted psychic environment that is conducive to producing the very best results, and with avoiding the need to constantly guard or protect themselves in the conduct of this work. As Morya forcefully stated, "Please realize the fact that so long as men doubt (our existence) there will be curiosity and enquiry... but let our secret be once thoroughly vulgarized and not only will skeptical society derive no great good, but our privacy would be constantly endangered and have to be continually guarded at an unreasonable cost of power."[7] One need only conjure a mental image of today's aggressive "paparazzi" mercilessly harassing celebrities and those in the news to acknowledge the truth of this assertion.

Stated succinctly, among the foremost reasons for the reclusivity, reticence, and silence of the Adepts and high initiates of the Order is to ensure the efficiency and efficacy of results of the work they do for humanity, primarily through their spiritual powers. None of this work can be done efficiently while expending "an unreasonable cost of power" to fend off avaricious and selfish curiosity, as Morya declared. And this strict conservation of spiritual energy is more than a consensus view of an obvious truth: it is a *rule* of their Order, stated in these terms and emphasis by KH, who wrote of "... the RULE that forbids our using one minim of power until every ordinary means has been tried and failed..."[8]

Inextricably related to the need for the highest efficiency and efficacy of their labors achievable in their pristine isolated environments, like the flip side of the same coin, is the added difficulty for highly purified Adepts to work in the mire and psychic pollution of the transient world they prefer to avoid. It is not that they are *unable* to do this, but more that they are *unwilling*, for cogent and justifiable reasons. One need only imagine a champion swimmer who swims quickly across a mountain lake of the purest water when, upon reentering the lake to swim back, he finds its contents have mysteriously turned into thick sugar cane molasses. How quick or efficient by comparison would be his return swim in those conditions, and how much greater an expenditure of energy would be needed? This aquatic physical metaphor has a metaphysical correspondence, being the purified Adept laboring in the toxic psychic miasma of the transient world as described in what follows by HPB, who minces no words:

> Sometimes, under very favorable conditions they [Adepts] may approach an individual devoted to occult research, but this happens rarely; for even he, pure though he be, is wallowing in the world's corrupt *akasa* or magnetic aura and contaminated by it. To his inner self it is as stifling and deadly as the heavy vapor of carbonic oxide to his physical lungs. And, remember, it is by the inner, not the outer, self that we come into relations with Adepts and their advanced Chelas. One would not expect to hold improving conversation with a besotted inebriate, lying in a state of swine-like stupefaction after a debauch; yet it is quite as impracticable for the spiritualised Mahatma to exchange thoughts with a man of society, living daily in a state of *psychic intoxication* among the magnetic fumes of its carnality, materialism, and spiritual atrophy.[9]

If this description by HPB is insufficient to convince anyone who would question it, any such doubts should be assuaged by a first-hand account of an Adept. KH retired from the outer world for several months in 1881-82 to take another advanced initiation (referred to by Morya as entering *Tong-pa-ngi*, a Tibetan term for "void") in a remote location in the Himalayas. After returning to his former labors around March of 1882 in a highly purified state, he found the readjustment painful. He wrote that "Since my return I found it *impossible* for me to breathe—even in the atmosphere of the *Headquarters!* [of The Theosophical Society in Adyar, India] M. had to interfere, and to force the whole household to give up meat; and they had, all of them, to be purified and thoroughly cleansed with various disinfecting drugs before I could even help myself to my letters."[10] Given the reclusivity, reticence, and silence they usually observe, and the distance they prefer to keep from psychic pollution, all in order to do their work with maximum efficiency and efficacy, Adepts should not be made to suffer the strain of sacrificing these preferences in order to train *chelas*—yet at times they do. When that occurs, what then do *chelas* owe in return?

If the first duty of a probationer or newly accepted *chela* ascending the higher spiritual path could be reduced to a single word, that word might well be "purification." This is because a sort of chasm exists between the purified and spiritualized environment within which the Adepts live and work, and the correspondingly lower or denser environment of the transient world in which the probationer or newly accepted *chela* typically lives, even if within an ashram or monastery.

Putting aside momentarily the delicate process of synchronizing the personal electromagnetic emanations or "frequencies" between *guru* and *chela*, it should not be for the Adept to have to adapt to the lower environment or world of the *chela*; it should be for the probationer or newly accepted *chela* to strive in adapting to the higher spiritualized environment of the Adept and other high initiates. And this is done by a conscious, unremitting and resolute process of *purification* leading to a refinement of his or her electromagnetic energies. KH stated simply that "... we invariably welcome the new comer; only, instead of going over to him he has to come to us."[11] "To come to us" is another way of saying that the *chela* must become fit, or qualified, for entry into that higher psychic environment by attuning his or her spiritual magnetic emanations to those of the Adepts and their world. Especially in these ominous times, this is not an easy task.

While this process of spiritual purification can be described as a task, it is more than that. It is a law, or duty, inherent in the time-honored tradition of the *guru-chela* relationship at this level of higher spiritual development. HPB cites the "Laws" of Upasana, or chelaship: "From Book IV of *Kiu-ti*, chapter on 'the Laws of Upasana,' we learn that the qualifications expected in a *chela* were: 1. Perfect physical health; 2. Absolute mental and physical purity..."[12] On the higher spiritual path this process of "absolute" purity, or purification, has two discrete modes: that which should be acquired and integrated by the wayfarer, and that which should be avoided.

As to the first of these modes, KH listed basic practices that further the process of purification which have been undertaken by spiritual aspirants since time immemorial. "Fasting, meditation, chastity of thought, word, and deed; silence for certain periods of time to enable nature herself to speak to him who comes to her for information; government of the animal passions and impulses; utter unselfishness of intention, the use of certain incense and fumigations for physiological purposes..."[13] More can certainly be added to this list of largely physical purification practices, such as following a plant-based diet, daily exercise, proper hygiene, and a regimen of *hatha yoga* including both normal *asanas* and the cleansing practices known as *shatkarmas*, which consist of six whole-body techniques. For guidance in undertaking a corresponding regimen of absolute mental purification, the most accessible for the wayfarer are the profound initiatic rules set forth in the 1885 book by Mabel Collins, entitled *Light on the Path*.

As to the second of these modes, or that which should be avoided, the list is even longer, especially for those living in the West. For the wayfarer on the higher spiritual path, the process of physical purification includes avoidance of the basic somatic distractions, such as poor diet and/or habitual overeating, sexual misconduct if not sexual relations altogether, and the use of intoxicants like alcohol and drugs—such as opiates—that constrict or contract the consciousness. One might also add here the avoidance of *all* related addictions or addictive behaviors that affect the body in a deleterious way.

By contrast, avoiding the psychic impediments to absolute mental purity is generally more difficult for the wayfarer than avoiding profligate physical behaviors. These impediments include, in the words of KH, "... furies called Doubt, Skepticism, Scorn, Ridicule, Envy and finally Temptation—especially the latter..."[14] One could add to this list the psychic impurities of avarice, dishonesty, egotism, mendacity, and the lust for power or for recognition or fame, all of which are wholly incompatible with ascending the higher spiritual path, to say nothing of chelaship. These are the types of moral or mental human foibles that not only invariably lead one to physical activities that ought to be avoided, but they invade the mind and often haunt one's meditation as inner monologues or as dialogues with others, and as vitiating daydreams.

These two modes of purification—what to acquire and what to avoid—and whatever other means may be employed to effect purification, must ordinarily be applied during the wayfarer's period of probation before accepted chelaship. Probation is normally a period of seven years, and throughout this time the probationer must face the challenges of absolute purification on his or her own, since as KH notes, "... until he has passed that period, we leave him to fight out his battles as best he may..."[15] The reason for this degree of reticence once again reaches back to the issue of a higher spiritualized environment of the Adepts, which in turn impels their preference to wait until the pupil is sufficiently purified before direct interaction between *guru* and *chela* can commence. This interaction involves a sensitive process of synchronizing the personal electromagnetic frequencies or emanations between *guru* and *chela*. "[I]n each case," wrote KH, "the instructor has to adapt his conditions to those of the pupil, and [for the Adept] the strain is terrible, for to achieve success we have to bring ourselves into a *full* rapport with the subject under training."[16] It took that long even for one of the founders of The Theosophical Society to achieve, for as KH further notes, "Olcott's magnetism after six years of purification is intensely sympathetic with ours—physically and morally is constantly becoming more and more so."[17]

For Adepts, the field of subtle electromagnetic emanations surrounding an aspiring *chela*—his or her aura—is not an intellectual construct, but rather an empirical reality. The more pure and less polluted that aura is, the greater the chance of further interaction with the Adept. But as in the case of Henry Olcott, it took at least six years, and that was with the constant tutelage of his *guru*, Morya. In most such cases, as KH pointed out, "The process of self-purification is not the work of a moment, nor of a few months, but of years—nay, extending over a series of lives."[18]

Regarding the present state of the spiritual evolution of humanity, the conflicting impulses that guide its course are in full tension. The modern world appears to be a creature that stubbornly refuses either to save or even to help itself. Everywhere we witness dislocation, political tumult, autocratic oppression, aggression, fear, incertitude, and suffering on a vast scale. Correspondingly, a visible and ever greater mass inversion of principles and values is afoot—too often good now yields to evil, truth yields to disinformation and falsehood, sustainable stewardship yields to exploitation, and so on. These lamentable inversions come with a heavy price, which we pay in global chaos and pollution, including pandemic diseases. The wayfarer on the higher spiritual path who recognizes the immediate need is duty-bound to help reverse this trend. The most effective way for the wayfarer to accomplish this is by aligning himself or herself with the Order of Adepts and high initiates, and their principles and values. And the *only* way this can be done is through a rigorous and sustained process of self-purification.

At stake is nothing less than whether humanity will soon become so spiritually unfit as to decimate its own multiple habitats on this globe—physical and metaphysical—by refusing to yield to the evidence and probity of spiritual evolution and unconditional love. And whether humanity will be able to succeed in reversing this trend may in part depend on whether enough probationers and newly accepted *chelas* are of sufficient fitness, or purity, to join the herculean struggle to reverse course and to move toward the light, rather than away from it. If not, then among the dire consequences humanity faces is one announced by KH: "If, for generations we have 'shut out the world from the Knowledge of our Knowledge,' it is on account of its absolute unfitness; and if, notwithstanding proofs given, it still refuses yielding to evidence, then will we at the end of this cycle retire into solitude and our kingdom of silence once more."[19]

3

Reincarnation and the Higher Spiritual Path

The night kissed the fading day with a whisper: "I am death, your mother, From me you will get new birth."
— Rabindranath Tagore

Among the subjects the spiritual wayfarer who is earnestly and resolutely treading the higher spiritual path must master are the qualities and composition of the *seven principles* of the human being. A clear understanding of these principles explains much, not only about the seven human states of being, but about all to which these states correspond in the metaphysical planes in which they operate. Necessarily included in this important and comprehensive subject is the *precise* configuration of those particular principles, in whole or part, that comprise the reincarnating entity within the human being—the "transmigrant." For the wayfarer, ever greater precision in understanding the constituent nature of this transmigrant and the specific human principles of which it is comprised, is both an indispensable and unavoidable requirement.

This essay examines (i) the composition of the principles of the decedent at the point of his or her death, including those of the inner transmigrant as it passes through this fatal ordeal, and (ii) the transmigrant's eventful journey through the various *post-mortem* states to rebirth. The method employed in this examination is that of sacred or *spiritual science* drawn largely from the writings HPB and two of her teachers, the Adepts Morya and KH. This spiritual-scientific method relies on the aggregated knowledge gained through observations of such spiritually advanced Adepts over millennia. Not only are many of these Adepts able to navigate and fully understand the most

31

subtle modalities of nature—the multiple states of being—and transmit their knowledge to their *chelas* and others, but some are able to traverse the journey between death and rebirth in a *fully conscious* state, and so relay this experiential knowledge as well.

The wayfarer pursuing greater precision of understanding might begin his or her inquiry by considering the question posed by HPB in 1884, when she asked—and answered—the following interrogative:

> NOW, what is it that incarnates? The occult doctrine, so far as it is given out, shows that the first three [of seven] principles die more or less with what is called the physical death. The fourth principle, together with the lower portions of the fifth, in which reside the animal propensities, has *Kama Loka* for its abode, where it suffers the throes of disintegration in proportion to the intensity of those lower desires; while it is the higher *Manas, the pure man,* which is associated with the sixth and the seventh principles, that goes into *Devachan* to enjoy there the effects of its good *Karma,* and then to be reincarnated as a higher individuality.[1]

It is the cumulative esoteric or theosophic data of spiritual science, and the knowledge derived from it, that comprises what will help the wayfarer fill in the interstices of HPB's answer above.

No thorough or detailed understanding of the transmigrant or of reincarnation as a process can be achieved without first having a clear or "scientific" understanding of the seven principles of the human being, a fact that bears repeating. This science is the classic *scientia* of the perennial philosophy. And just as the physical or hard sciences of today employ as their basic epistemological tool the "empirical" method based on the perceptions of man's five senses—and the technology that enhances their observational powers—so too are the subjects and processes of the metaphysical planes regarded as empirical realities by those Adepts who have perfected their latent powers and are thus able to study them *in situ*.

It should also be noted that in addition to transmigration and the *post-mortem* states, spiritual science also includes other domains of spiritual or psychic development. Specifically, these other predominantly metaphysical domains pertain to the functioning of the primary nerve plexuses or *chakras*, the ancient developmental methods known as *kundalini yoga* and *prānāyāma*, and generally the development and use of *siddhis* (powers) through the affirmative activation of the *chakras*, which include clairvoyance, clairaudience, and telekinesis, among others. The seven principles of the human being, we hasten to add, play as central a role in these domains as they do in the processes of death and rebirth—reincarnation.

The higher of the seven principles of the human being can best be understood by reference to Sanskrit terms in the Vedantic formulation of the five (*pancha*) constituent *kośas*, or "bodies" (alternatively translated as "sheaths" or "vehicles" or "envelopes") as found in the Taittiriya Upanishad. We can add to these translations the English word "principles," being HPB's and the Adepts' term of choice. The three highest *kośas*, sometimes referred to as the "higher triad," are the *ānandamaya-kośa*, which may aligned with *ātmā*; the *vijñānamaya-kośa*, which may also be understood as *buddhi*; and *manomaya-kośa*, often termed the *manas*. The Vedantic *ātmā-buddhi-manas kośas* align exactly with the three higher principles used by HPB, Moyra, and KH, and these writers consistently follow the order in their writings that the *ātmā*, *buddhi*, and *manas* are the 7th, 6th, and 5th principles, or *kośas*, respectively. In succinctly summarizing this doctrine of principles, Morya stated that "Man has his seven principles, the germs of which he brings with him at his birth."[2]

The "lower quaternary," or the lower four of these seven principles, does not lend itself to corresponding comparisons of the term *kośa*, described above. Rather, these lower principles appear as *sharīras*, also translated as "body," in the Katha Upanishad. *Sharīra* is another Sanskrit term which, though semantically different from *kośa*, is used in the classic designation of subtle vehicles or envelopes, and similar translations. The Katha Upanishad identifies three *sharīras*, only two of which are used in the theosophic septenary designation of principles. *Sthūla-sharīra*, is the gross physical body and first of the septenary principles. *Linga-sharīra*, the 2nd principle, is an astral counterpart or "double" of the physical body comprised of *ākāśa*, which HPB describes as "super-sensuous spiritual essence which pervades all space." The 3rd principle, composed of *fohat* energy, is consistently referred to as *jivatma*, or "life principle," by the 19th-century theosophical writers. Similarly, the 4th lower principle is referred to as the *kama-rupa*, and is the center of desire, emotion, and volition. Thus, during incarnate life, in each person the seven principles operate as a cohesive unit until death, yet are functionally bifurcated as "lower quaternary and higher triad" owing to the fact that these two are, respectively, mortal and immortal, and also designated as the Lower or Outer Person and the Higher or Inner Person.

One important if not crucial observation about these principles needs highlighting, which is that the 5th principle— *manas* or mind—is itself bifurcated between the lower mind, the seat of ordinary thoughts, and the higher mind, the seat of abstract and/or spiritual thought. In esoteric literature these two aspects of *manas*, sometimes referred to as *rupa* (formal, or lower) and *arupa* (formless, or higher), are separated by a subtle divide known as the *antahkarana* that "bridges" the lower and higher minds. For our purposes it is necessary to understand that for most decedents during the *post-mortem* journey, the highest portions of *manas* being the *manas arupa*, along with certain "sublimated essences" from other lower principles, "join" the 6th and 7th principles (*buddhi* and *ātmā*) to comprise the transmigrant.

Another key component to understanding precisely what it is that reincarnates is clearly understanding the relationship between the 7th and 6th principles, or *ātmā* and *buddhi*. While these principles may be key to a clear understanding, they are also the most difficult to describe, owing largely to the fact that *ātmā* is infinite, unconditioned, and eternal and therefore not subject to any contraries or to any limitations that may be ascribed to it by language, or even by thought. To grasp or apprehend even an approximation of this principle, the faculty of reason must be surpassed, and the intuition that operates in human beings by and through the *buddhi* can provide the only feasible understanding. But because the *ātmā* and *buddhi* are two discrete and separate principles, they deserve to be discussed separately.

The *Ātmā*: "We include Atma among the human 'principles,'" wrote HPB, "in order not to create additional confusion. In reality it is no 'human' but the universal *absolute* principle of which Buddhi, the Soul-Spirit, is the carrier."[3] This permanent, immortal non-human attribute applies only to the *ātmā* among the seven principles. All the rest are impermanent, though it should be kept in mind that the 6th principle and the higher 5th principle are lasting companions of the *ātmā* throughout the entire course of its transmigration in the material realm until its re-entry into the paranirvanic state, and only then disintegrate. Quoting the Parinirvana Sutra, KH states that "... it is only when all outward appearances are gone that there is left that one principle of life [*ātmā*] which exists independently of all external phenomena. It is the fire that burns in the eternal light, when the fuel is expended and the flame is extinguished; for that fire is neither in the flame nor in the fuel, nor yet inside either of the two but above, beneath, and everywhere."[4] He then adds a critical distinction that "... neither Atma nor Buddhi were ever *within* man..." The profound significance of this simple phrase cannot be overstated.

Further quotes from HPB in describing *ātmā* nonetheless seek to describe the ineffable in words: "The seventh [is] the synthesis of the six, and not a principle but a ray of the Absolute ALL—in strict truth;"[5] and "Ātma is nothing; it is all absolute, and it cannot be said that it is this, that or the other... It is simply that in which we are;"[6] and "The Higher Self is Ātma, the inseparable ray of the Universal and ONE SELF. It is the God above, more than within, us."[7]

The Buddhi: In its passive condition, the 6th principle or *buddhi* is, in HPB's words, the "vehicle," the "carrier," and even the "casket" of the *ātmā* or 7th principle. We say "passive" condition because *buddhi* is said to have both a passive and active condition. This is explained by KH in his observation that "The supreme energy resides in the Buddhi; latent [*i.e.*, passive]—when wedded to Atman alone, active and irresistible when galvanized by the *essence* of 'Manas' and when none of the dross of the latter commingles with that pure essence to weigh it down by its finite nature."[8] HPB adds that "It is Buddhi considered as an active instead of a passive principle (which it is generally, when regarded only as the vehicle, or casket of the Supreme Spirit, Atma)."[9] Because *buddhi* has this dual active-passive aspect, and can be galvanized by the essence of the 5th principle, *manas*, it is mutable and ultimately impermanent, unlike the *ātmā*. This conclusion is supported by HPB, who wrote that "The sixth Principle in Man (Buddhi, the Divine Soul) though a mere breath, in our conceptions, is still something material when compared with divine 'Spirit' (Atma) of which it is the carrier, or vehicle."[10]

Notwithstanding the unconditioned and omnipresent nature of the *ātmā*, there is yet an enigmatic *individuality* about it that is core to the nature of the transmigrant as a whole, including its *buddhi* and the sublimated essences it has assimilated from prior incarnations. Based on what has so far been said of the *ātmā*, this assertion sounds almost like a contradiction in terms, if not a fallacy. Yet HPB boldly addressed this suprarational if not mystic concept by venturing to say that "... though merged entirely into Parabrahm, man's spirit [*ātmā*] while not individual *per se*, yet preserves its distinct individuality in Paranirvana..."[11] While rationally inexplicable, this preservation of a "distinct individuality" throughout the entire transmigration of the spiritual Monad from beginning to end is nonetheless the only explanation for the ability of the Adepts, and certain others, to recollect at will—and accurately—the entirety of all their past incarnations on earth. HPB helps explain this by noting that "The most spiritual—*i.e.*, the highest and divinest—aspirations of every personality follow *Buddhi* and the Seventh Principle [*ātmā*] into Devachan (*Swarga*) after the death of each personality along the line of rebirths, and become part and parcel of the *Monad*," or the one and only transmigrant.[12]

Beyond the fates of the 1st, 2nd, and 3rd mortal principles at the time of death, and the destinies of the 6th and immortal 7th principles, it only remains to follow the varying outcomes for the 4th and 5th principles in the *post-mortem* states. Once the lowest three principles have died together at the moment of death, and thus have separated from the remaining higher four principles, the 4th and 5th principles then coexist temporarily with the 6th and 7th principles in the *kama-loka* until a "struggle" occurs between them. For understanding this interactive struggle, we refer to KH's description of it:

Thenceforth it is a "death" struggle between the Upper [6th and 7th principles] and Lower [4th and 5th principles] dualities. If the upper wins, the sixth, having attracted itself the quintessence of *Good* from the fifth—its nobler affections, its saintly (though they be *earthly*) aspirations, and the most

37

Spiritualised portions of its mind [5th principle]—follows its divine *elder* (the 7th) into the "Gestation" State; and the fifth and fourth remain in association as an empty *shell*...[13]

Like the 1st through 3rd principles that all die together at death, the 4th and 5th principles—having lost the karmic struggle with the 6th and 7th principles and thus temporarily existing as a "shell"—will also gradually dissolve in the *post-mortem* states. This dissolution occurs after the *manas* or 5th principle has rendered to the *buddhi*, the 6th principle, those sublimated essences or "spiritual spoil" of the 5th principle that will then follow or join the *buddhi* and will thereby become absorbed by the reincarnating entity—the transmigrant. KH refers to that which follows or joins the 6th principle or *buddhi* into *devachan*, and thereafter to rebirth, as "the quintessence of *Good*" from the 5th principle, as its "nobler affections," as its "saintly aspirations," as its "spiritual spoil," and as its "most spiritualized portions." HPB refers to the same thing as the "most spiritual—*i.e.*, the highest and divinest—aspirations," not of the 5th principle *per se*, but of every "personality." She adds, speaking specifically of the "'higher attributes' of the 5th principle," that the "... noblest higher feelings—such as undying love, goodness, and all the attributes of divinity in man, even in their latent state—are drawn by affinity towards, follow and merge into the monad [transmigrant], thus endowing it... with a personal self-consciousness..."[14]

Accounts provided by the Adepts and HPB regarding this mystic following or joining or assimilating elements (or essences) of the 5th principle into the 6th principle in *kama-loka*, first describe aspects of the *manas* or mind of the decedent that qualify for survival and rebirth. But there is yet another element or essence to consider in this process of merging or following or assimilation. Arising within the 4th principle and thus understood as feelings, or emotions, by initiates of the Order of which the Adepts are members, love and hatred are described by KH as *"immortal* feelings." As such, they appear to be an exception to the rule that all those components comprising the 4th of the seven principles of the human being—the *kamarupa* or the seat of emotion—disintegrate in the *kama-loka* at some point after death.

KH further explains that no other feelings in the bliss of *devachan* exist "... outside that immortal feeling of love and sympathetic attraction whose seeds are planted in the fifth, whose plants blossom luxuriantly in and around the fourth, but whose roots have to penetrate deep into the sixth principle..."[15] The higher 5th (*manas arupa*) and 6th (*buddhi*) principles are the "spiritual faculties" noted by KH in this further clarification: "Out of the resurrected Past [prior incarnation] *nothing* remains but what the Ego [transmigrant] has felt *spiritually*—that was evolved by and through, and lived over by his spiritual faculties—be they *love* or *hatred*."[16] It is significant that KH uses the verb "felt" to explain the resurrection of love in the *postmortem* state of *devachan*, in contrast to exclusively 5th-principle intellectual aspirations or recollections arising from a human being's prior spiritual milestones.

While the transmigrant consists primarily of the 7th and 6th principles, the *ātmā* and *buddhi*, the transmigrant *also* contains portions of the higher 5th principle (*manas arupa*) together with these sublimated elements or essences arising from the two immediately lower principles. Most of these essences arise from our highest intellectual spiritual aspirations and the impersonal love and compassion we exhibited during our incarnate lives. No specific name or term is given to these "assimilated" elements or essences by the Adepts or HPB. But HPB did mention that, in addition to containing what has already been described about them, they contain a necessary *self-conscious* awareness of the individuality of the transmigrant which does not exist within either the 7th or 6th principles. They would also contain a metaphorical ledger of karmic considerations from prior incarnations to which the transmigrant is subject.

We thus have a transmigrant composed of the 7th and 6th principles, *plus* some surviving essences integrated into the higher 5th principle or *manas arupa* that follow or are assimilated into the 6th principle. When this aggregate of whole and partial surviving principles is fully synthesized, it provides both self-consciousness and a preferred destination for the transmigrant to navigate in its succeeding incarnation.

In summary, the seven principles of the human being are commonly divided as (i) the higher three or "higher triad," and (ii) the lower four, or "lower quaternary." The lowest principle of the "higher triad," being the 5th principle or *manas*, is further subdivided into two portions, the *manas rupa* (lower) and the *manas arupa* (higher). Further, little to nothing of the ordinary mind, *manas rupa*, reincarnates, but rather eventually disintegrates along with the 1st, 2nd, 3rd, and 4th principles in the process of *post-mortem* transition. Conversely, either some portions or most of the *manas arupa*, together with certain purified essences or distillation of experiences, follow or "join" the 6th principle or *buddhi* and collectively these with the 7th or *ātmā* comprise the reincarnating entity or transmigrant. This conclusion comports exactly with a parallel statement made by HPB, where she refers to the transmigrant as "the higher individuality": "In short, the higher individuality of man, composed of his higher *Manas*, the sixth and the seventh principles, should work as a unity, and then only can it obtain 'divine wisdom,' for divine things can be sensed only by divine faculties."[17] Based on the foregoing it might therefore be more accurate to view the higher and lower division of the seven principles as between the lower 4½ (lower four plus *manas rupa*) and 2½ (higher two plus *manas arupa*). But as tempting as it may be to codify the transmigrant simply as the higher part of a 4½ to 2½ division of the seven principles, it is not so simple.

The most difficult, most inscrutable, and least described aspect of the transmigrant in the literature of spiritual science is this aggregation of sublimated essences or distillations of one's previous incarnation(s) arising from the 4th and 5th principles, which then follow or join the 6th principle. We have seen what both KH and HPB stated about this arcane process: that what of the decedent's 5th principle follows or joins the *buddhi* in the *post-mortem* states are "the quintessence of *Good*," "nobler affections," "saintly aspirations," "spiritual spoil," "most spiritualized portions," "highest and divinest aspirations," and "all the attributes of divinity in man," *etc*. But the analysis does not end here. There is, in addition, the matter of specific "immortal *feelings*" arising in the 4th principle, the feelings of only love and hatred, to use the words of KH. By virtue of being immortal, at least up to the point of liberation, these feelings—or at least that of love—must also survive the *post-mortem* transition and join the *buddhi* as an integral part of the reincarnating entity, the transmigrant.

We begin toward formulating an actual definition of the transmigrant, therefore, with what is certain and clear: The immortal 7th principle (*ātmā*) together with its carrier the 6th principle (*buddhi*), which both "overshadow" the incarnate person but are never "within" him or her, are the two basic and constant principles that comprise the transmigrant. We then add to these two principles some part of the higher 5th principle or mind, the *manas arupa*, which is added by means of a "joining" with the *buddhi*. This 5th composite principle so assimilated or joined to *ātmā-buddhi* contains within it the most spiritual or divine portions of the combined *manas* together with *only* impersonal and unconditional love as a feeling or emotion, arising from the 4th principle. Within these conjoined essences are the further characteristics of self-conscious awareness, and an access to past incarnations which, when merged or assimilated into the *buddhi*, support HPB's notion cited above

41

that "... man's spirit while not individual *per se*, yet preserves its distinct individuality [through *ātmā*] in Paranirvana." We believe it is these highest spiritual essences surviving from the 4th and 5th principles merged into the 6th principle that allows this "distinct individuality" until the point of liberation from the wheel of death and rebirth is achieved, after which only undifferentiated *ātmā* remains. If, then, we were to ascribe a term to that part of the transmigrant that was neither the 6th nor 7th principle, we might use "sublimated spiritual essences" arising from the 4th and 5th principles. But one must take care in formulating such a definition *not* to suggest that any mundane or ordinary portion or segment of the 4th or 5th principles, unrefined and non-spiritual, survives to join the *buddhi* as part of the transmigrant.

Based on all the available data of spiritual science, we believe the "transmigrant" may be defined in this way: *the overshadowing and immortal 7th principle or ātmā within its carrier the 6th principle or buddhi, joined through the latter by a portion of the higher 5th principle containing certain "sublimated spiritual essences" arising from the 4th and 5th principles.* It is mostly by virtue of the differing spiritual essences of human beings that each transmigrant differs. Pristine oneness lies alone in the *ātmā*. The individual transmigrant retains self-conscious awareness and recollection throughout its reincarnations until it achieves liberation as a *jivanmukti*, after which no other principles will remain after death and dissolution except the one non-human 7th principle, *ātmā*.

As regards the spiritual wayfarer, this eventual outcome just described above will differ for those who consciously elect to defer *nirvāna* to follow the path of the *bodhisattva*. So, the *desideratum* of a wayfarer on this higher spiritual path, especially where he or she has come within the precincts of probation or chelaship of an Adept in the present incarnation, is never to pause or to change course upon rebirth, but rather to advance farther along this same path in the succeeding incarnation. Instructive here is HPB's observation that "Pre-existing or *innate* virtues, talents or gifts are regarded as having been acquired in a previous birth."[18] As quick a resumption as possible of ascending the higher spiritual path following his or her rebirth ought to be seen by the wayfarer as such a "virtue, talent or gift," grounded in the hard work and sacrifice of advancing on this path in prior incarnations. To achieve this outcome, the wayfarer must use as indispensable tools a thorough knowledge of the seven principles of the human being, of the specific composition of the transmigrant, and of the entire *post-mortem* transition from death to rebirth in this universal process of transmigration.

4

Karma and the Higher Spiritual Path

Karma neither punishes nor rewards; it is simply the one universal LAW which guides unerringly all other laws productive of certain effects along the grooves of their respective causations.
– H.P. Blavatsky

In June of 1884, Henry Olcott received a letter from one of his spiritual teachers, the Adept KH, and among the statements KH made to Olcott was this: "You have talked a great deal about karma but have hardly realized the true significance of that doctrine."[1] The context of this letter makes clear that KH was addressing not just Olcott, but the collective of spiritual seekers and prospective *chelas* around him, as well. If this discrepancy between having "talked a great deal" yet having "hardly realized" much about the true significance or doctrine of karma among esotericists was obvious to KH in the year 1884, this discrepancy applied to the wider public in our time would exceed that of 1884 by a hundredfold. This is because today "karma" has become popularized as a fashionable cultural form, and as such has largely been divorced from its traditional spiritual definition and usage. As this trend has gradually occurred over the last 150 years, the meaning of karma has become ever more diluted and misunderstood as a spiritual concept—not so much among wayfarers or esotericists generally, but certainly among the wider public in the West.

Among the necessities of ascending the higher spiritual path is the wayfarer's need to realize, in KH's words, the "true significance" of the law identified by the Sanskrit word *karma*. The necessity of such a realization is based in the simple truth that karma represents a core or "first principle" of the *philosophia perennis,* upon which the operations if not the meanings of other first principles, such as that of periodicity, for example, rely for their own universal applications.

There are at least two useful methods or tools for the wayfarer to employ in achieving a realization of karma's true significance. The first method is that while the law of karma is actually multivalent, it is more easily understood as dualistic. This dual perspective entails a personal and an impersonal application; a corresponding physical and metaphysical application; and a corresponding application best described as a lower mind or 5th principle (*manas rupa*) perspective, and a higher mind or 5th principle (*manas arupa*) perspective infused with the light of the 6th principle or *buddhi.* This last "manasic" application can be stated otherwise as a (i) rational intellectual and a (ii) suprarational intellectual perspective. A focus on this first method, or tool, comprises the preponderance of the content that follows in this essay.

The second such method or tool, being yet another confirmation of the multivalency of the law of karma, is simply recognition by the wayfarer that different names are given to this law. In the writings of HPB and her principal teachers, the Adepts Morya and KH, these names represent different features, applications, and thus valencies of this law, and so we see the "Law of Karma" variously and otherwise referred to in their writings as: "the Law of Retribution,"[2] "the Law of Compensation,"[3] "the Law of Re-adjustment,"[4] and "the Law of cause and effect."[5] Each of these separate designations—and others from different sources, including the "law of mediate causes"—points to a different branch stemming from the trunk of the tree of karmic law. KH observed that "We have several sorts of Karma and Nirvana in their various applications—to the Universe, the world, Devas, Buddhas, Bodhisatwas, men and animals—the second including its seven kingdoms."[6] This assertion is given additional support by the observation of HPB that "Karma is a word of many meanings, and has a special term for almost every one of its aspects."[7]

These two wayfarers' tools, to summarize, are the (i) awareness of the multiple names and modes of operation of karma, and a (ii) reduction of these plural modes into a simpler dualistic approach for meaningful understanding—personal and physical on the one hand, and impersonal and metaphysical on the other. Equipped with these tools, the wayfarer on the higher spiritual path is the more empowered to make good progress toward compliance with the implicit exhortation of KH's words to Olcott about the need to realize the "true significance" of the law of karma.

Before proceeding to examine any higher or spiritual dimensions of our subject, it is important for several reasons to take further note of the extensive popularization of the term karma in the West, and its effects. We focus here on the West, rather than any global popularization of the term, owing to the variations of meaning of karma in the East—in Asia—where it has been imbedded in those cultures for millennia owing to its salient presence as a core religious precept in both Hinduism and Buddhism. By contrast, in the West, in its popularized form karma has devolved into a concept that has been largely desacralized as a spiritual principle, and predominantly portrayed as a sort of inscrutable cosmic retaliation against bad actors who arguably deserve punishment.

Perhaps as consequences of (i) the mission of HPB and H.S. Olcott begun in the late 19th century, which brought to the attention of many in the West the salience of the *philosophia perennis* within ancient religions of the East, and of (ii) the wide and rapid dissemination of the same principles of yoga and Eastern religions that occurred in the West in late 1960s, today karma has nearly become a "household" word. The term has found its way into the cultural mainstream and often appears in scripts of film and television productions, and in media literature of the day. This infusion of the term karma into popular Western culture has brought with it a corresponding obscuration of the term's deeper meanings, thereby prompting widespread misunderstanding of its true spiritual and cosmic meaning, or significance.

In popular culture the desacralized term karma has come to be cloaked in a patina of retaliation, rather than divine retribution, perhaps through long-term cultural absorption of a command set forth in *Leviticus* 24:20: "Breach for breach, eye for eye, tooth for tooth: as he hath caused a blemish in a man, so shall it be done to him again." Such a strict approach as this to restoration of balance is primarily a societal mechanism aimed at behavior and obedience, and largely divorced of spirituality. In fact, it is a literal exegesis of the ancient law of retaliation (*lex talionis*, the "claw of the law") whose operational principle, known as disambiguation, is that a person who has injured another must be penalized in the same way, or closely similar, as suffered by the injured party. Predating the Old Testament, the earliest recorded expression of this ancient concept is found in the *Code of Hammurabi*.

Having now noted this popularization, and desacralization, of the term karma in the modern West and its extensive misuse as essentially retaliative—though occasionally tinged with a hue of the mysterious—it need detain us no further. Any such vernacular uses of the term karma comprise no portion of the stated subject of this essay, so we may now turn our full attention to the topic at hand, being the operation of karma within the context of spirituality.

Little disagreement exists among scholars of Sanskrit that the basic translation into English of the term karma is "action," as an executed "act," though one occasionally finds the English words "deed" or "work" as translations. This same basic translation is also widely accepted by esotericists, with respect to the term's root meaning in Sanskrit, as evidenced by a definition provided by Ananda Coomaraswamy, being "action, by thought, word, or deed." He adds, "In its simplest form, this doctrine merely asserts that actions are inevitably followed by their consequences, 'as a cart a horse.'"[8] This is further supported by HPB's basic definition: "Karma *(Sk.)*. Physically, action: metaphysically, the LAW OF RETRIBUTION, the Law of cause and effect or Ethical Causation."[9] Elsewhere she states that "Karma thus, is simply *action*, a concatenation of *causes* and *effects*."[10] Yet the simplicity of this term as so translated belies the complexity of its application, especially as it relates to the spiritual, or metaphysical, realm.

The most scientific illustration of the cause-and-effect nature of the principle of karma as action in the material realm can be observed in Isaac Newton's third "law of motion," published in *Principia* in 1687: "To every action there is always opposed an equal reaction: or, the mutual actions of two bodies upon each other are always equal, and directed to contrary parts." Not only does this succinct and eloquently stated law of physics properly relate action (karma) to motion, but it leads inescapably to the further conclusion that "reaction" is the co-equal counterpart to action and, as such, must therefore necessarily fall under the plenary principle of action-as-karma, as well.

In all realms, therefore, karma covers equally *both* action and reaction. This is because reaction, though it may be contingent upon ingenerate action, is nonetheless action itself, and together an action and its reaction form a unit within a concatenation, or linked "chain" of actions. This observation leads to higher and suprarational dimensions of karma that will be addressed momentarily. But here we acknowledge this rational and impersonal facet of karma in its physical application as a motor propelling all phenomenal action/reaction, that may be described alternatively as the motion or flux between the poles of duality, or polarity—another core or first principle of the *philosophia perennis*.

It is probable that the application of karma most familiar to esotericists is the personal one, which pertains to individual transmigration, or reincarnation. Certainly the law of karma applies to human beings in an *intra*-transmigrational sense, meaning that the reaction to some action done by someone in his or her early life may manifest at a later point in the same incarnation. But the most common usage, if not understanding, of karma by many if not most esotericists refers to its *inter*-transmigrational sense—that is, the law of karma applied to the effects of specific actions as spanning multiple incarnations. It is in this sense that karma is frequently discussed by HPB and the Adepts. "The law of KARMA," wrote HPB, "is inextricably interwoven with that of Re-incarnation."[11] This is because, as HPB also noted, "... *Karma* or action is the cause which produces incessant rebirths or 'reincarnations.'"[12]

Based on these established principles, the Adept Morya explained that "Now every individuality will be followed on its ascending arc by the Law of retribution—Karma and death accordingly."[13] And so, consistent with these fundamental and rational propositions of the theosophical doctrine, the spiritual Monad or "transmigrant" reappears in flesh at the dawn of each new incarnation—at least up to its last involuntary one when it has achieved liberation from the wheel of death and rebirth. And there, in that luminous dawn, "The law of retribution as *Karma*, waits man at the threshold of his new incarnation."[14]

One further or additional observation must be made regarding *all* the karmic effects that "await man at the threshold of his new incarnation." These karmic effects are not those caused solely by the individual, or ourselves. Rather, we must *each* bear the weight of the oppositive—as distinct from positive—karma caused by those with whom we associate, or even those in our larger vocations, castes, ethnicities, or nationalities. Speaking metaphorically of blows to the individual by a "sword" in the "hand of karma," HPB claims there is "... one [blow] for the transgressor, the other for the family, nation, sometimes even for the race, that produced him."[15] This *collective* view of karma is one that HPB repeats in numerous places, and one which is confirmed by KH who declared that "It is a true manhood when one boldly accepts one's share of the collective Karma of the group one works with, and does not permit oneself to be embittered..."[16]

To this point, what has so far been discussed is fundamentally a restatement of the law of karma as understood by many, if not most, esotericists. Yet for those wayfarers ascending the higher spiritual path, the dive into this profound doctrine must go even deeper to realize its "true significance," to repeat the words of KH. The depths upon which the law of karma rests, and from which it draws meaning like some desert tree whose taproot reaches meters below to a life-giving aquifer, is the metaphysical principle of *causality*, whose most prominent profile is often expressed as "cause and effect." As a point of beginning, one can see an equivalency if not a correspondence between the concepts of (i) action and *cause*, and (ii) reaction and *effect*, but this is essentially a launching point for the discussion that follows.

The question of causality, or HPB's related term "ethical causation," relative to the concept of karma may be said to be both semantic and metaphysical. Even if suprarational in scope, the verbal equation "action: cause:: reaction: effect" is by no means a nonrational or illogical proposition. If one accepts this equation as valid, both the concept and definition of karma should then necessarily involve the first principle of cause and effect—or causality. Ananda Coomaraswamy provides a passage which conveniently incorporates the interaction of these first principles. He explains the Sanskrit term *pitryāna* within a specific traditional context, being in this case the mythic story where *pitryāna* was represented as the "Patriarchal Voyage" (transmigration) of the "Pilgrim" (spiritual Monad). Alluding to this entire patriarchal voyage by the pilgrim, Coomaraswamy wrote:

> In other words, the *pitryāna* is a symbolic representation of what is now called the doctrine of reincarnation, and is bound up with the notion of latent (*adrsta* or *apūrva*) causality. The purely symbolic character of the whole conception is made all the more apparent when we reflect that from the standpoint of very Truth, and in the absolute Present [eternal Now, or aeviternity], there can be no distinctions made of cause and effect; and that what is often spoken of as the 'destruction of *karma*,' or more correctly as a destruction of the latent effects of Works, effected by Understanding and implied with *mukti*, is not really a destruction of valid causes... but simply a Realization of the identity of 'cause' and 'effect.'[17]

Here Coomaraswamy uses the terms "latent causality" and "the latent effect of Works" interchangeably, "cause" being replaced in the second term by "Works," work being one among several words used for translations of the Sanskrit word karma. This brings into alignment the metaphysical first principles of "cause and effect" and its corollary "action and reaction" with *causality*, which traces its roots to the depths of the Absolute, and so can be said to have both absolute (latent) and relative (active) aspects. It is within this hieratic sphere of understanding that wayfarers on the higher spiritual path will be able to realize, borrowing once again the words of KH, the "true significance" of the doctrine of karma, especially as that relates to the coincidence of opposites.

Fully consistent with this view is that of HPB who, in describing karma as "one with the Unknowable," states that "Karma is an Absolute and Eternal law in the world of manifestation; and [] there can only be one Absolute, as One eternal ever-present Cause..."[18] While it is not possible to conceive intellectually from the standpoint of Unknowability, one can conceptualize the initial process of emergence or manifestation from the Absolute as duad from monad, and further conceive of the various ways in which this duad has functionally become bifurcated in manifestation. One of those ways appears as relative causation, or cause and effect, and another is or appears as the first principle of polarity, which is the cosmic—and terrestrial—stage upon which action and reaction, of cause and effect, both play. The law of karma inheres in these twin aspects of relative causality, and "adjusts" imbalances in the activity of the links connecting action and reaction, cause and effect. Without this crucial adjustment, there would be only chaos manifesting as eternal imbalance and disequilibrium.

In this drama which contains both cosmic and individual levels, the interaction/interplay or flux of action and reaction, of cause and effect in between the opposite poles of duality, can be seen as a fluidic motion. To repeat HPB's words, this fluidic motion is "*action*, a concatenation of *causes* and *effects*." Karma, or action, thus includes the "action of linking" or the "linking process" in the theosophic perception of the chain of causes and effects, restated here by Coomaraswamy: "The traditional and orthodox [Vedantic] doctrine is a recognition of the causal chain by which all events are *linked* in a phenomenal succession, but of their intrinsic and not extrinsic operation."[19] In other words, viewed from *extasis* or duality (or multiplicity) and differentiation, this process is seen objectively as a kinetic chain of innumerable causes with innumerable effects both through the universe and in our lives. But viewed from *enstasis* or inherent unity and wholeness through the suprarational perception, this process may also be understood as a singular impartite Cause, in which no distinctions can be made between cause and effect or action and reaction, because these opposites have become coincident in the perception—and in the life—of the enlightened viewer.

It is this view from *enstasis* that wayfarers on the higher spiritual path should ultimately seek to achieve—a permanent vision of *coincidentia oppositorum* (the "coincidence of opposites") within action, a transcendence of the contraries that are the progeny of the principle of polarity. It is also a direct application of this view to the wayfarer's sentient life that should also become an objective to be achieved, which is the coincidence—or perfect balancing—of his or her positive and oppositive karma, achievement of which bestows liberation and the Sanskrit title of *jivanmukti*. Such extraordinary achievements by the wayfarer will necessarily include full realization of the "true significance" of the law of karma. It will also comport with the view of HPB when she observed that "Once an Arhat obtains full illumination and perfect control over his personality and lower nature, he ceases to create 'merit and demerit' [or karma]."[20]

Initiation is conferred upon those wayfarers who are able to reach the summit of the higher spiritual path through these achievements of harmony and balance, among others. At that point, as a new initiate, a consequential choice is made after which his or her way typically becomes the way of the *bodhisattva*. Also at that point his or her deeper understanding of the *philosophia perennis*, of *theosophia*, including the doctrine of karma, will impel this initiate to actualize the compassionate directive of the Mahachohan to "Teach the people to see that life on this earth, even the happiest, is but a burden and an illusion, that it is but our own *karma*, the cause producing the effect, that is our own judge, our Saviour in future lives, and the great struggle for life will soon lose its intensity."[21]

5

Consciousness and the Higher Spiritual Path

The disciples of Gautama always awake well-enlightened. Their consciousness, by day and night, delights in contemplation.

– Dhammapada (Canto XXI)

"Everything in the Universe," wrote HPB, "throughout all its kingdoms, is CONSCIOUS: *i.e.*, endowed with a consciousness of its own kind and on its own plane of perception."[1] The wayfarer who treads the higher spiritual path should not only accept this premise as true, but should further understand the active operational aspects of *human* consciousness "on its own plane" as a means to achieve initiation, ultimately followed by illumination, or liberation, and release from the cycle of death and rebirth. The greater the expansion of the wayfarer's individual consciousness, the closer he or she comes to the *reintegration* of that individual consciousness with what HPB referred to as cosmic consciousness.

Just as universal or cosmic consciousness emerging from the Absolute has its septenary division, so does relative or individual consciousness. All formal manifestation that emerges in the immense periodic cycles comprised of what in Sanskrit are known as *manvantaras* has this septenary design, originating from the undifferentiated latency of their counterparts known as *pralayas*, into which former *manvantaras* have dis-integrated. This septenary design reflects an ancient principle, and one which is repeatedly affirmed throughout the writings of HPB. One salient example of her repeated affirmations is a concise article in an 1883 issue of *The Theosophist* devoted to and titled "The Septenary Principle in Esotericism." The views HPB expressed on this subject were echoed by the Adept KH, who wrote that "As man is a seven-fold being [with seven "principles"] so is the universe—the septenary microcosm being to the septenary macrocosm but as the drop of rainwater is to the cloud from whence it dropped and whither in the course of time it will return."[2]

While it may be simplistic to state that the relation of the septenary divisions among universal and individual consciousness is akin to the relation between the abstract and the concrete, these latter terms nonetheless indicate a corresponding similarity regarding this relationship. More specifically, HPB wrote that "The three upper are the three higher planes of consciousness... the lower ones represent the four lower planes—the lowest being our plane, or the visible Universe. These seven *planes* correspond to the seven *states* of consciousness in man."[3] Again we encounter the principle of correspondence expressly stated in her exposition. The sevenfold nature of human consciousness is, in principle, a septenary subset of relative or individual consciousness, and that, in turn, is a septenary subset of universal or cosmic consciousness, which nicely illustrates the patterns inherent in the law of correspondence.

There is thus an unbroken line, a nexus, that runs through all levels of manifestation as a septenary pattern. From macro to meso to micro, and return, one constant and recurring theme is this "septenariness." But the correspondences are just those, and should not be understood as exact, fractal replicas or facsimiles of one another on these various levels. While a septenary pattern is constant, there is variation in the nature and qualities of the plane or state at issue. It is important to note here that HPB carefully distinguished between the seven corresponding *planes* of individual consciousness and *states* of human consciousness in her statement above. She herself emphasized these two words with italics. Following this same choice of words, HPB refers in a diagram of consciousness in *The Secret Doctrine* to "... the four lower planes of Cosmic Consciousness, the three higher planes being inaccessible to human intellect as developed at present. The seven states of human consciousness pertain to quite another question."[4]

In esoteric philosophy, also known as the *philosophia perennis*, the human being and human consciousness are evolutionary spiritual "works in progress." In our investigation of consciousness we must maintain a mindfulness that our brains and our minds are currently somewhere in the middle of their ultimate cyclic development as that pertains to "rounds" and their spiritually evolutionary and cyclic subdivisions of extraordinary duration. Therefore, what we say about them here applies only to our present stage. According to HPB human consciousness currently consists of "... our seven states of consciousness—*viz.*, (1) waking; (2) waking-dreaming; (3) natural sleeping; (4) induced or trance sleep; (5) psychic; (6) super-psychic; and (7) purely spiritual—[that] corresponds with one of the seven cosmic planes..."[5]

Among the core issues or perspectives that separate the esotericist and the secular humanist, for example, is whether the brain or the consciousness is *a priori*. For the esotericist, the conclusion that arises from this inquiry is simple: in the largely Sanskrit terminology that applies, in order *first* there is Spirit (Brahman/*ātmā*), then universal intelligence (*mahat*), then consciousness (*prajña*), and then the physical brain. Secular humanists, and others, hold that just the reverse is the proper order: that intelligence and consciousness—excluding altogether the Spirit—are essentially epiphenomena of the brain, which is first. The esoteric perspective was articulated by KH when he wrote that "We do not bow our heads in the dust before the mystery of mind—for we *have solved it ages ago*. Rejecting with contempt the theistic theory we reject as much the automaton theory, teaching that states of consciousness are produced by the marshaling of the molecules of the brain..."[6] HPB was similarly adamant in scorning the "high priests" of science, as she described them, of the 19th century for seeking simply to "... resolve consciousness into a secretion from the grey matter of the brain..."[7] The true simplicity of this Spirit (*ātmā*) vs. mind (*manas*) debate about priority was captured by Ananda Coomaraswamy in his repeated criticism of the materialist view contained in René Descartes' axiom "*Cogito ergo sum*," (I think, therefore I am). Coomaraswamy called this axiom a "*non sequitur*," and sought to correct it simply by reversing the words as "*Sum ergo cogito*," (I am, therefore I think), with the emphasis being on the first "I" as the spiritual *ātmā*, reflecting the ancient maxim "I Am That" (Sanskrit, *so'ham*).

Modern neurology establishes that different parts of the human brain are responsible for different functions, and HPB made special mention of the pineal gland, which produces a serotonin-derived hormone called melatonin. She asserts that "The special organ of consciousness is of course the brain, and is located in the aura of the pineal gland in the living man."[8] And speaking esoterically, not anatomically, she added that at least during the incarnate existence of the person, the pineal "... gland is in truth the very seat of the highest and divinest consciousness in man, his omniscient, spiritual and all-embracing mind."[9] That being the case, then the other process, *i.e.*, ordinary rational thought, which normally occurs in the frontal lobe of cerebral cortex, performs functions like language, reasoning, and practical cognition.

This separation of the primary operations of human consciousness being linked to two discrete locations of the physical brain strongly suggests a corresponding bifurcation inherent in a core doctrine of the seven principles of the human being, of which the three highest are the 7th or *ātmā* (Spirit), the 6th or *buddhi* (intuition), and the 5th or *manas* (mind) in their Sanskrit names. And to repeat, this core doctrine pertains to a bifurcation in the last of these three principles, *manas*, into (i) ordinary or rational cognition, known as the *manas rupa* (formal, or lower mind) and (ii) abstract or spiritual thought, known as the *manas arupa* (formless, or higher mind), these two aspects of *manas* being separated by a subtle divide known in Sanskrit as the *antahkarana*.

These dual operations of the brain function—frontal lobe/pineal gland, and *manas rupa/manas arupa*—are further reflected in a dual operation of human consciousness or, as HPB phrases it, a "double consciousness." As to the ordinary and rational waking consciousness, HPB explains that "... the 'brain-self' is real while it lasts, and weaves its Karma as a responsible entity. Esoterically explained it is the consciousness inhering in that lower portion of the Manas [*rupa*] which is correlated with the physical brain."[10] She refers to this lower type of human consciousness as "sentient" consciousness, and contrasts it to the "spiritual" consciousness. The sentient consciousness is derived from the "lower manasic light," or *manas rupa* which dies with the body at death. The spiritual consciousness is derived from the *manas* "illumined by the light of Buddhi," or *manas arupa*, which in part survives the death of the body. As HPB further explained,

> There is a spiritual consciousness, the Manasic mind illumined by the light of Buddhi, that which subjectively perceives abstractions; and the sentient consciousness (the lower *Manasic* light), inseparable from our physical brain and senses. This latter consciousness is held in subjection by the brain and physical senses, and, being in its turn equally dependent on them, must of course fade out and finally die with the disappearance of the brain and physical senses.[11]

Death of the human being marks the end of the person's "sentient consciousness" in that particular incarnation, since the brain—

including its pineal gland—dies with the physical body. This is the departure of the phenomenally based consciousness of the mortal *manas rupa* from the noumenally based consciousness of the surviving portion of the *manas arupa*, joined with and bound to the higher *buddhi* and its immortal *ātmā*. That which remains of the person is solely the "spiritual consciousness"—of the *ātmā-buddhi-manas arupa*—after death. This is because "... the ideas about the infinite and the absolute are not, nor can they be, within *our* brain capacities. They can be faithfully mirrored only by our Spiritual consciousness..."[12] Moreover, such spiritual ideas and concepts within whose spheres we might find the attribute of *self*-consciousness (*ahamkāra*) would similarly be mirrored by our spiritual consciousness. "For, in the act of self-analysis," HPB wrote, "the *Mind* becomes in its turn an object to the spiritual consciousness. It is the overshadowing of the Mind by *Buddhi* which results in the ultimate *realization of existence*—i.e., self-consciousness in its purest form."[13]

For millennia various esoteric associations of seekers of truth, and systems or schools of yoga, all proffering similar spiritual practices, have existed in conformation with the immutable and immemorial principles of the *philosophia perennis*, or *theosophia*. Such schools and associations have taught and practiced a variety of methods and techniques to attain enlightenment, or liberation. Together with esoteric denominations and traditions within the world's major religions, these schools and associations collectively provide diverse spiritual paths which, at their highest levels, merge into a uniform initiatic path. What is central and common to virtually all these traditions is some form of contemplative meditation, usually as a daily practice of gradual self-control or mastery of the mind through focused concentration by application of the will. Meditation is universally *key* to advancement upon the higher spiritual path, and to the expansion of consciousness.

Culturally infused meditative practices of the East, such as *zazen* of the Mahāyāna Zen Buddhist schools (including those of Japan, China, Korea, and Viet Nam), or *vipassanā* of the Theravāda Buddhist forest traditions, or *lojong* of the Vajrayāna Buddhists, or classical *rāja yoga* of traditional Hinduism have, in our time, become global. Occasionally these practices are conflated with sitting while reciting *mantras*, or *japa*, as in Hinduism, or with the practice of *dhikr* among Islamic Sufis, or even with the customary practice of repetitive recitation in Christian hesychasm. These recitative practices are also sometimes conflated with prayer, which is not meditation. While it may be true that the Eastern meditative practices can be valuable portals of entry to meditation for those in the West, taking a purely sacred science and non-denominational approach to the subject of meditation in terms of the seven principles of human beings provides far more clarity, particularly as to those principles to which we refer as *ātmā* (the 7th), *buddhi* (the 6th), and *manas arupa* (the higher 5th).

Without purposefully trying to do so, HPB virtually defined the goal of meditation in sacred science terms by her quote above in stating that "It is the overshadowing of the Mind by *Buddhi* which results in the ultimate *realization of existence*..." To expand this statement as applied to meditation, we can respectfully add that it is the intentional objective of overshadowing the *manas* or 5th principle of the practitioner by the *buddhi* or 6th principle that eventually leads, through daily and sustained practice, to deep and prolonged meditative or *jhāna* states, *i.e.*, to the ultimate realization of existence. This practice involves the calm stilling of all (lower) mental activity followed by a sustained concentrated focus upon a single point of (higher) spiritual significance which, stated alternatively, amounts to a temporary cessation of "sentient consciousness" in favor of "spiritual consciousness," to use HPB's terms.

Among the initiates and Adepts of KH's order, meditation is acknowledged as an ancient and indispensable practice for spiritual development and progress upon the higher spiritual path. To repeat, as KH noted on this precise subject, the daily practice of "Fasting, meditation, chastity of thought, word, and deed; silence for certain periods of time to enable nature herself to speak to him who comes to her for information...," will in time allow spiritual aspirants to achieve "illumination."[14] And, turning to Buddhism, this same Adept quoted the Theravadin *Mahavāgga* of the *Khandhaka*: "When the real nature of things becomes clear to the meditating Bhikshu, then all his doubts fade away since he has learned what is that nature and what its cause." KH then added to this a comment of his own: "Meditation here means the superhuman (not supernatural) qualities, or arhatship in its highest of spiritual powers."[15]

It should not be surprising that, in relation to other world religions, Buddhism is so often consulted in inquiries about meditation or, for that matter, about consciousness. It is fair to say, to explain this tendency, that no other religion approximates the scope or level of discourse about meditation as is found in Buddhist scriptures. This fact may now introduce the Buddhist *jhāna* states of meditation or, more accurately, of consciousness, since they are nothing less than the manifestation of the vertical axis of consciousness which ascends hierarchically from lowest to highest. Appearing and repeated in a number of the early *suttas* of the Pāli canon, the higher *jhāna* states are the meditative planes reached by advanced practitioners of meditation which effectively describe expansions of awareness, or of consciousness. Among those *suttas* most often quoted is the *Samyutta Nikāya* (45:8), verses 8-10, which reads as follows:

And what, monks, is right concentration? Here, monks, secluded from sensual pleasures, secluded from unwholesome states, a monk enters and dwells in the first jhāna, which is accompanied by thought and examination, with rapture and happiness born of seclusion. With the subsiding of thought and examination, he enters and dwells in the second jhāna, which has internal confidence and unification of mind, is without thought and examination, and has rapture and happiness born of concentration. With the fading away as well of rapture, he dwells equanimous and, mindful and clearly comprehending, he experiences happiness with the body; he enters and dwells in the third jhāna of which the noble ones declare, 'He is equanimous, mindful, one who dwells happily.' With the abandoning of pleasure and pain, and with the previous passing away of joy and dejection, he enters and dwells in the fourth jhāna, which is neither painful nor pleasant and includes the purification of mindfulness and equanimity.[16]

This text is an explication of one feature of the "eightfold path" in Buddhism, being "right concentration" or in some translations "right meditation," which is found in the last or fourth of the "Four Noble Truths" of the Buddha. What should be understood is that no bright or clear lines exist between these *jhāna* states that the practitioner encounters during meditation. Rather, they should be understood as truth of the existence of higher and more subtle levels of one's inner journey that merge into one another as the wayfarer progresses in meditation and, for that matter, on the higher spiritual path.

The pinnacle of meditation, and affirmative spiritual development generally, can be conceived by the Sanskrit word *samādhi*, whose detailed treatment is found in the *Yoga Sutras of Patañjali*, among other texts. This state of elevated consciousness is not easy to describe, surpassing as it does the conceptions of the rational mind and the vocabulary that mind uses. But we attempt to do so nonetheless by using the words of HPB above, with slight modification. She refers to the overshadowing of the *manas* or 5th principle of the practitioner by the *buddhi* or 6th principle, and when this occurs through sustained concentration and will by the practitioner, *both* these principles, the 5th and 6th, become effectively illuminated by the divine emanations of the 7th principle, the *ātmā*. When the mind is focused and at last in alignment with the *buddhi*, then can the mind be illuminated or enlightened by the immortal *ātmā*. This is the state of *samādhi*.

At the same time, it is an illumination of the human consciousness. Stated alternatively by KH, "It is, when correctly interpreted, in one sense 'the *divine Self* perceived or seen by [personal] *Self*,' the *Atman* or seventh principle ridded of its *mayavic* distinction from its Universal Source—which *becomes the object of perception for, and by the individuality centered in* Buddhi, the sixth principle, something that happens only in the highest state of *Samadhi*."[17] And this statement by KH is affirmed by HPB when she wrote about Plotinus' definition of "real ecstasy" as "the liberation of the mind from its finite consciousness, becoming one and identified with the infinite," and adding that "It is, indeed, identical with that state which is known in India as Samadhi."[18]

This essay ends as it began—by quoting from the writings of HPB: "Individual consciousness emanates from, and returns into Absolute consciousness, which is eternal MOTION."[19] The effect of reaching the *samādhi* state is crossing the bridge that connects and thus allows a return to—a reintegration into—universal or cosmic consciousness from individual consciousness. It is full circle, where the mouth of the ouroboros consumes its own tail in the endless spiral of eternal motion. But for the individual human being who has attained or achieved this highest level, which allows this permanent reintegration of individual consciousness, there remains a choice. This choice is whether to release that individual consciousness back into the cosmic consciousness via *nirvāna*, as the "dewdrop slips into the shining sea" so eloquently conveyed by Edwin Arnold, or to *defer* this reintegration and continue incarnate as a conscious light-bringer on behalf of humanity. This latter is the path of the *bodhisattva,* where the high initiate may learn to transfer his or her individual consciousness "unbroken" from death to rebirth. As HPB explains, "Those alone, whom we call adepts, who know how to direct their mental vision and to transfer their consciousness—physical and psychic both—to other planes of being, are able to speak with authority on such subjects."[20]

Thus is one's individual—and illuminated—consciousness put to practical use for the benefit of humanity, in order to assist in the sacred mission of the Order of Adepts, which mission is none other than the spiritual enlightenment of humanity as a whole. In this endeavor the new *bodhisattva,* likely an initiate in that Order, learns in time to "become exempt from the curse of UNCONSCIOUS transmigration."[21] Once this ability is mastered, the initiate then has "Complete or true immortality, which means an unlimited *sentient* existence, [that] can have no breaks and stoppages, no arrest of *Self*-consciousness."[22] In the same context, HPB writes that "Immortality is but one's unbroken consciousness..."[23] This individual *unbroken* consciousness, where voluntarily not released and thus not reintegrated into the cosmic consciousness, is wholly present in a person—a *bodhisattva*—who compassionately sacrificed this reintegration and the eternal bliss of *nirvāna* that accompanies it. For so serving first the needs of humanity, of such a person it can be said, "Immortal then is he, in the *panaeonic* immortality whose distinct consciousness and perception of *Self under whatever form* undergoes no disjunction at any time, not for one second, during the period of his *Egoship*."[24]

6

Expanded Use of Will on the Higher
Spiritual Path

[T]here is no Impossibility to him who WILLS.
– H.P. Blavatsky

Though the exact date is uncertain, sometime around the year 1883 S. Ramaswami Iyer, a South Indian man and an accepted *chela* of the Adept Morya, wrote to his *guru* with the following question: "Will it be for my good, and will it assist me in the development in me of my clairvoyant and clairaudient powers, if I every morning between 4 a.m. and 6 a.m. keep a pin of iron before me and try to move it by my will power?" Morya responded to his *chela's* question with these words: "TRY; it can do no harm, and may assist. M."[1]

It is likely that for those unfamiliar with esotericism and the development of certain latent powers known in Sanskrit as *siddhis*, the image created in their minds of Mr. Ramaswami sitting at a desk in the early predawn hours intently focused on a pin and trying to move it about by will power might evoke a sense of bemusement, if not comedy. Yet for those students of the esoteric doctrine who are serious aspirants determined to ascend the higher reaches of the spiritual path, including the possibility of initiation into that august company of those known as Adepts, and their *chelas*, the development and use of the will is no laughing matter. Rather it is, along with development and use of the intuition, an indispensable condition for further progress along that higher spiritual path.

The available material on the development and use of the will is voluminous, so in what follows this sizeable subject must be compressed into its most pertinent and succinct formulation, with the objective that it may be found practically useful. Accordingly, a brief discussion at the outset is needed to place "will" in its universal or cosmological context, and to observe its imprint in manifestation or formal creation, including its subsequent appearance in the composition of the human being. Thereafter the discussion focuses on two principal uses of will on the higher spiritual path. Though one could label these two uses of will in various ways, *omission* and *commission* are as heuristic as any. Thus, will used in the sense of *omission*, or as self-control, first controls and then eradicates (omits) the desires, passions, and attachments of the Outer Person that impede the sacred ascension of the Inner Person, and access to the higher reaches of the spiritual path. Will used in the sense of *commission* can create, by means of its limitless power, tangible results in virtually all the planes of nature, including the mundane. This use of will as commission, however, carries with it a solemn caveat of strict karmic consequences for the serious spiritual aspirant wherein he or she must always carefully avoid injecting any *personal* goal, desire, or ambition that animates or clouds or contaminates this use of will.

In defining the term "will," HPB wrote that "In metaphysics and occult philosophy, Will is that which governs the manifested universes in eternity. *Will* is the one and sole principle of abstract eternal MOTION, or its ensouling essence." In the same definition, HPB then discusses the form and process of its manifestation:

> Like all the rest, the Will is *septenary* in its degrees of manifestation. Emanating from the one, eternal, abstract and purely quiescent Will (Âtmâ in Layam), it becomes Buddhi in its Alaya state, descends lower as Mahat (Manas), and runs down the ladder of degrees until the divine Eros becomes, in its lower, animal manifestation, *erotic* desire. Will as an eternal principle is neither spirit nor substance but ever-lasting ideation.[2]

It is clear from this definition that will, as a subject of inquiry, includes the totality of theosophic metaphysics from creation and everlasting ideation to the use of its power by individuals both to overcome the multiple temptations of earthly life and to effect actual results, from the ordinary and routine to the production of occult phenomena.

Elsewhere, will is described by the Adept Morya as "... the Universal *Sakti*—the Will-Force, or universal energy...,"[3] and by his brother KH as a central part of the "all-pervading supreme power" which "... is exactly matter, whose life is motion, will, and nerve power, electricity." KH follows this description with this useful aphorism: "Purush [spirit] can think but through Prakriti [matter]."[4] These descriptions of will, taken together, provide that nothing exists in the manifested universe that does not involve or implicate will in some degree or other, on every level of existence. And significantly, HPB equates the inherent creative will of "animated beings" to existence of the "organic frames of their bodies" and especially their "voluntary actions," among other things. She thus articulates the connection between the vast galactic macrocosmic modality of the principle of will, and the microcosmic or individual *human* modality of will which includes direct application of will as action upon contingent circumstances. The same creative will power that also engenders these circumstances, or phenomena, is that which is "... identical with what we find in ourselves and call— WILL."[5]

"Will power" and "will force" are both terms of strength which denote, through "power" and "force," that once harnessed and controlled by the resolute wayfarer on the higher spiritual path, this power is real and can be enormous depending upon the inner strength of the wielder of such will. Solely for purposes of clarity, will has already been bifurcated into types or uses as omission and commission, which correspond to what can amount to using will both as a shield and as a sword, provided that in using the latter it must be used by the spiritual wayfarer only to protect and help others. Thus, the use of will as omission is effectively its use as a shield, defending against and permanently repelling (omitting) the relentless onslaught of "... furies called Doubt, Skepticism, Scorn, Ridicule, Envy and finally Temptation—especially the latter..."[6] with which one living in this material world is confronted daily. These "furies," so named by KH, are among the impediments—since there are many more—that confront aspirants for probation and even chelaship under an Adept and that *must*, by the force of their individual wills, be eradicated in order for the wayfarer to proceed farther along this path.

These and other related "furies" of the human psyche, or character, are extraordinarily powerful. As a brisk wind propels and steers fallen leaves, these "furies" often effectively propel and steer the lives of most human beings who are either unaware of or unconcerned with the existence of an initiatic path of spiritual unfoldment. Moreover, in the case of a probationer or even a new *chela*, all of these furies do not diminish in number or strength. Rather, as a *consequence* of probation or chelaship, these furies become re-energized and hyperactive—bigger and bolder—so that the strength of self-will needed to defend against them must necessarily be correspondingly greater. This is so because both the struggle, and the stakes, for these spiritual aspirants reach new levels of gravity as they steadily advance.

To name but a few, these furies or desires consist of attachments to material comfort, sensate pleasures, prestige, and hunger for wealth or power within the outer world. These urges and others like them are the tools, or agents, of the metaphoric "Dweller" on the threshold between mortality and immortality, corresponding here to the Outer Person and the Inner Person. These agents mercilessly assault the wayfarer, who by using only his or her will, can shield himself or herself from the subtle deceits and overt aggression that are among the methods of the Dweller to preclude the wayfarer from progress on the higher spiritual path. "For he who hopes to solve in time the great problems of the Macrocosmal World and conquer face to face the Dweller, taking thus by violence the threshold on which lie buried nature's most mysterious secrets, must Try, first, the energy of his Will power, the indomitable resolution to succeed...".[7]

These last four words bear repeating, because they comprise a succinct and useful definition of "will," whether used in the sense of omission or commission. "Indomitable resolution" is *resolve* that is both powerful and entertains no doubt, no room for failure. Such resolution is put to the test when the wayfarer resolves to cease or refrain from engaging in any behavior inimical to his or her higher spiritual development. Such behaviors are, for example, envy of those who have more; unrestrained acquisition of wealth or excess property; scorn for those with whom he or she disagrees; desire for recognition or fame; leveraging of power over others; or temptation by pleasures from unhealthy foods to easy money to sexual misconduct. Only where that resolution is endowed with a complete absence of doubt that it will succeed, shall the wayfarer wield his or her will (in the sense of omission) in a way that can "conquer face to face the Dweller" and all such behaviors. Doubt is poison to the use of will, and to one's resolve, invariably maiming or entirely destroying the will's objective.

Before turning our attention to the use of will in the sense of commission, a final and important thought needs to be added to the discussion of the use of will in the sense of omission. This thought comes in the form of a warning from HPB, and concerns the difference between (i) merely deflecting or suppressing these "furies" within us, and (ii) eradicating them altogether with finality. Perhaps as an antidote to what she saw as illegitimate curiosity about certain schools of *tantra* of her time—a curiosity that has only grown with time in our own era—she warned as follows about how best to deal, and not to deal, with one's desires and animal passions on the spiritual path:

> There are those whose reasoning powers have been so distorted by foreign influences that they imagine that animal passions can be so sublimated and elevated that their fury, force, and fire can, so to speak, be turned inwards; that they can be stored and shut up in one's breast, until their energy is, not expanded, but turned toward higher and more holy purposes... For this purpose they will not struggle with their passions nor slay them. They will simply, by a strong effort of will, put down the fierce flames and keep them at bay within their natures, allowing the fire to smoulder under a thin layer of ashes.[8]

In the final analysis, such deflection or suppression of these passions is a mistake, she argued. "It is only when the power of the passions is dead altogether," wrote HPB elsewhere, "and when they have been crushed and annihilated in the retort of an unflinching will; when not only all the lusts and longings of the flesh are dead, but also the recognition of the personal Self is killed out and the 'Astral' has been reduced in consequence to a cipher, that the union with the 'Higher Self' can take place."[9] Let the wayfarer be on notice, then, to realize that use of the will in omitting the "furies" from his or her constitution is comprised of more than simply suppressing or deflecting them with a shield as a warrior of old might have deflected arrows and clubs. Rather let the wayfarer be on notice that these furies must be omitted from his or her inner constitution *forever*, with no chance of reappearance, by having been annihilated in the fiery retort of the will.

Unless comatose or otherwise similarly afflicted, every living human being uses will in the sense of commission every day, simply to do the most basic and ordinary things. Before these things are accomplished, the individual must decide or elect to do them, and then put forth some degree of will, or energy, or motion, to carry out this decision—this thought. The same ordinary process of using will by the populace at large also includes the wayfarer, though he or she may, in ascending the higher reaches of the spiritual path, begin to use the will in a more *extraordinary* process of commission—as would a true *bodhisattva*. As to this wayfarer, and to all those becoming proficient in the occult sciences, the use of will in this sense takes on an entirely new and vastly expanded dimension.

In addition to other terms describing this extraordinary process, one may also refer to the expanded dimension of this use of will as *magic*. "Paracelsus," wrote HPB, "teaches that 'determined will is the beginning of all magical operations. It is because men do not perfectly imagine and believe the result, that the (occult) arts are so uncertain, while they might be perfectly certain.'"[10] KH wrote that "Imagination as well as will—creates."[11] To work properly as a function of the Intellect, the imagination must create as perfect an image or idea as possible, whose clarity is not unlike a photograph or a painting by a surrealist artist like Dalí. Then, upon this image's *infusion* by the operator's will power, the image or idea acts as a sort of receptacle for the operator's will and so becomes energized and thereby *engendered* by that will power, after which it becomes an active or phenomenal "creation."

If, however, this mental image or idea of the Intellect is imperfect, or if there is any doubt in the mind of the operator infusing it that it can achieve activity and its desired effect, then it will likely fail altogether and disintegrate like some item of biodegradable mental refuse. But more problematically, if the new creation is only partial yet still active, its outcome may become dysfunctional and might even cause its creator difficulties, depending upon the degree of imperfection or doubt infused with the energizing will into the crippled creation.

While both the ordinary use of will as commission, and the extraordinary use of will as commission that we may call magic, are used in ascending the higher reaches of the spiritual path, it is the latter upon which we are focused here. Speaking precisely to this point, KH's senior *chela* Djual Khul wrote in a letter to a new *chela* about the operation of what he termed "Will-Essence," how it is "... transmitted from the operator to his objective point," and that "... you perhaps scarcely realize how everyone is practically, albeit unconsciously, demonstrating this law every day and every moment. Nor, can you quite realize how the training for adeptship increases both one's capacity to emit and to feel this form of force."[12]

Such increased capacity to emit this "force" or, alternatively stated, to utilize magic, was among the abilities HPB developed further in her own training. The production of various occult phenomena by HPB in the earlier years of her mission, such as the telekinetic precipitation of flowers and handwritten letters and teacups, for example, ultimately resulted in adversity in her later years. These actions, and the suspicions arising from them by the incredulous, formed the basis for excoriation of her character as fraudulent, as alleged in a report of the Society for Psychical Research published in 1885. HPB came to believe that ultimately such phenomena did adversely impact her mission, even though there was never any selfish or spiritually unethical motive in her use of will to produce these occult phenomena. But the unintended consequences that later unfolded in their wake illustrate the care that must be taken in using the will in this extraordinary way, even where the motives generating its use are pure and even compassionate.

The magical use of will as commission can be put to at least two extraordinary purposes: one operating on extrinsic objects and activities, and the other operating on the will of other beings. Where limited by being used only for the welfare of humanity and never oneself, the first of these purposes would clearly be consistent with the role of wayfarers, and with the roles of those who might teach them. Even where an aspirant fails in such a use of will, if the motive behind this use were selfless and compassionate, the result would not be irremediable.

The same, however, cannot be said of using one's will to control the will of another. Speaking of the accepted rules of the Order to which he belongs, KH stated that "We never try to subject to ourselves the will of another."[13] This because it is forbidden to Adepts by their own "... wise and intransgressible laws to completely subject to themselves another and a weaker will—that of free born man. The latter mode of proceeding is the favourite one resorted to by the 'Brothers of the Shadow,' the Sorcerers..."[14] Similarly, HPB decried those who "... send up waves of will-power for selfish or unholy purposes..." which she described as "... abomination, and spiritual sorcery."[15]

It should be evident in light of the above that oppositive consequences await him or her who misuses the will in the ascent to the higher reaches of the spiritual path. This fact is all the more important because of increases in the will's power that may occur in training along this path involving the development of certain of the primary *chakras*. Preferable is letting these force centers develop naturally and synchronistically, or through supervised training by a *guru* qualified to do so, corresponding to initiatic advancement of the individual on the higher spiritual path. In stark contrast to this method are those individuals motivated solely by a personal goal to develop these force centers as *siddhis*, thereby acquiring occult powers. It may be true that the power of one's will can be greatly increased on one's own through the unsupervised practice of methods like *kundalinī yoga*, which may be an irresistible temptation for some. But where such a practitioner who is not completely selfless and spiritually pure prematurely forces open these *chakras* for the purpose of attaining occult powers, it almost always amounts to a recipe for self-destruction. When such powers are forced too soon, it takes only the smallest fugitive grain of self-interest in an otherwise purified character to enable sliding backward down the hill of self-benefit on a slippery slope to sorcery, like a small snowball that begins rolling downhill which ultimately becomes a tremendous avalanche.

Either as omission or commission, the use of will is unavoidable for everyone alive, whether one pursues a normal or routine life, or an esoteric and extraordinary life ascending the summit to spiritual truth. As a practical matter, then, the wayfarer of this latter category may safely begin the development of will as omission, first by a rigorous and pitiless self-examination to identify his or her own deficiencies ("furies"), or impediments, to further spiritual growth. Having once identified such deficiencies, and perhaps beginning with lesser ones in order to gradually build confidence, let him or her then bring one by one *all* these furies to heel, and thereafter eradicate them altogether. In this endeavor, the risks are small and the reward great.

As to the development of will as commission—excluding entirely subjugation of the will of another—considerably more caution should be used by the wayfarer. This enters the realm of magic, where rushing headlong into this arena without being supervised by one who is fully qualified, is tantamount to navigating a minefield blindfolded. The risks here are greater, but if done properly the rewards for others—for humanity— may be commensurably greater. Yet this use of will might best be left for those who are prepared; that is, for those who have mastered their Outer Person by force of will as omission. Let us not forget that Mr. Ramaswami, in entering the practice of the use of will as commission by mentally focusing on moving about a pin, was under the supervision of an Adept as an accepted *chela*. His *guru* exemplified, as HPB wrote, a perfect mastery of both the use of will as omission and commission, and could unquestionably be described as "A man of profound knowledge, exoteric and esoteric, especially the latter; and one who has brought his carnal nature under subjection of the WILL; who has developed in himself both the power (*siddhi*) to control the forces of nature, and the capacity to probe her secrets by the help of the formerly latent but now active powers of his being..."[16] This is the sacred paradigm to which all on the farther reaches of the higher spiritual path ultimately aspire, particularly as it pertains to the use of the will. This will must be ever further developed—carefully, gradually, and lovingly— not only to continue ascending toward this consecrated tier of higher spiritual reality, but thereafter to apply toward the solemn *work* of bringing enlightenment to humanity.

Free Will in Light of the Higher Spiritual Path

No man is free who is not master of himself.
– Epictetus

Serious students of the immemorial wisdom tradition, the *philosophia perennis*, will be familiar with the issue of terminological complexity, if not outright confusion, in the study and comparison of certain core words and terms in express treatises of this philosophy in all venues and throughout all ages. Such sacred literature is written in Pāli and Tibetan, in Greek and Latin and Hebrew, and in the newer languages of French and English, to name but a few. The immutable truths of this immemorial philosophy were also recorded by the earliest Taoist and Vedic scribes of the ancient world in Chinese and Sanskrit, restated in numerous other later languages and, most recently, restated in extraordinary scope and detail in modern English by HPB and those for whom she served as agent.

The causes of this terminological complexity and/or confusion are multiple. The principal causes include, among others, variability of the spiritual insight of the original scribes, differing idiomatic and cultural metaphors used to explain subtle principles, and the linguistic abilities and esoteric expertise of translators of the written treatises and scriptures. Often due to such causes, terminological complexity and/or confusion were virtually endemic to these treatises and scriptures, especially where one undertakes comparisons between them. This is so notwithstanding that the core or first principles of the *philosophia perennis* are ever the same and unchanged, regardless of spatial or temporal considerations.

This terminological complexity/confusion not only has been but continues to be a challenge for many serious seekers—wayfarers—on the path of higher spiritual development. However, this problem is largely remediable with the justifiable conviction that the first principles themselves do not differ, but rather what differs are the terms and descriptions used in the fluidic oral and written languages in which these principles are memorialized. Stated most succinctly, the core principles of the *philosophia perennis* are immutable, but the various ancient and modern languages in which they were originally transmitted and later restated are mutable. And because a proper understanding of the term "free will" and its relation to the traditional doctrine of the "two selves" are key to ascending this steep spiritual path, this essay seeks to avoid any further complexity/confusion by attempting to provide greater analysis and clarity for those who seek.

Within the continuum of ancient and modern theosophic literature one has only to think of the wide variety of uses and meanings to which the English word "soul," for example, has been put. One need only refer to the rendering in other languages of terms that are translated into English as "soul"—the Greek *psyche*, for example—to find ambiguities in, and discrepancies between, both its definitions in and translations from those other languages. Even where each of numerous original writers of esoteric texts was referring to *exactly* the same principle or phenomenon as other such writers of different eras and venues, the terms employed by those writers in their own languages, and the varying synonyms and metaphors they used to define and clarify these principles, both enable and remain subject to recurring terminological complexity and/or confusion.

These primary problems of the original expositions then become further compounded, if not exacerbated, by secondary translations of these terms and descriptions into the mutable forms of communication we call language—from one language to another. This became highly apparent in the 19th and 20th centuries when a deluge of esoteric doctrines first written in early Asian and Indo-European languages began to be translated into modern European languages, including English. One has only to refer to the various and multiple translations of the Sanskrit term *dharma* (Pāli *dhamma*) to encounter a plethora of meanings for the same term.

Given this long list of factual predicates, before entering into a formal discussion of free will—a principle that has perplexed both students of esotericism and analytical philosophers alike—it is essential to identify as well as possible related terms that are necessarily incorporated into this discussion. A discussion of "free will" requires, at the least, some description if not definition of the term "will," together with the terms "choice," and "fate" (Latin *fatum*, from which *fatalis* is derived). It further requires familiarity with the principle of the two selves—the "Outer Person, or Man/Woman" (lower self) and the "Inner Person, or Man/Woman" (higher Self). These dual Outer (lower four) and Inner (higher three) composites of the human being are, effectively, a practical and useful shorthand reduction of the seven modalities or principles from which they are formed, known in Sanskrit as *kośas*, and translated variously as "subtle bodies" or "vehicles" or "sheaths" that correspond to the multiple states of being. To repeat here briefly what was discussed in greater detail above, if we adopt the classic Vedantic formulation of *kośas*, we may say that the highest three *kośas* or envelopes are the *ānandamaya-kośa*, which align with *ātmā*; the *vijñānamaya-kośa*, which may also be termed the *buddhi*; and that below these is the mind, or *manomaya-kośa*, often termed the *manas*.

Together these three highest of the *kośas* (*ātmā, buddhi, manas*)—or the 7th, 6th, and 5th principles, respectively—comprise what is referred to, for the purposes of this essay, as the Inner Person or higher Self. The remainder of the lower principles—

not enumerated here but including the physical and vital bodies, together with the subtle modalities where exist one's "personality" with its desires, appetites, and self-identity—comprise the lower self or Outer Person. This summary overview of the concept of the "two selves" (Outer-Lower/Inner-Higher) must for now omit any treatment of the crucial bifurcation of the 5th principle or *manas* into (i) ordinary versus (ii) abstract or spiritual thought, in order to better focus on a proper understanding of free will as understood in the traditional or perennial philosophy.

In order to understand what *"free* will" is, it is obvious that one must first understand what is meant by and understood as "will." The term will, like the term free will, is also subject to a multiplicity of meanings by modern, secular philosophers as well as by scientists of the mind/brain complex, from psychiatrists to neurologists. With no intention to be dismissive, we may refer to these modern and empirically based analytical inquirers into will and free will collectively as secularists, and so directly contrast them to esotericists, being the students and sages of sacred spiritual truths, variously recorded in known texts and treatises of the perennial wisdom tradition.

A principal difference between secularists and esotericists is the methods they use. The secularist typically relies on the faculty of reason alone, and allows as support fundamentally that which is quantitative and can be adduced empirically, and so typically rejects any notion of the Inner Person or spiritual component within human beings. This rejection, or at least the omission, of any reference to one's higher Self (*ātmā-buddhi-manas*) in the dialectic discourse and deliberations of the secularists, necessarily means that their conclusions pertain solely to the principles comprising one's Outer Person. This is the Outer Person of the physical body, its vital principle, the emotions and desires, and the lower mind, all of which describe the commonplace "identity," or "self-identity," and "personality" of the person that exists for *only* a single incarnation, until these mortal features all disintegrate at or near the moment of death, and shortly thereafter.

Conversely the esotericist, while accepting the reality of the higher Self yet *also* relying on the reason of the higher mind, further synthesizes this intellect with the intuition operating through the *buddhi* in order to fully understand a subject, including its qualitative nature. Though it is often worthwhile to familiarize oneself with any conclusions of secularists that may be cogent, it is important to keep in mind that where the initial premises used by secularists are solely quantitative and empirical, and the analyses of their subjects of inquiry are exclusively limited to logic and reason, so their conclusions must share in that process and thus be imbued with the same limitations. This being the case, the modern secularist would *ipso facto* not be able to accept—nor perhaps to understand—the idea of free will as perceived by great expositors of the wisdom tradition.

Within the context of these dual categories, as an esotericist HPB formulated a precise definition of will. "Will," she wrote, "is that which governs the manifested universes in eternity. *Will* is the one and sole principle of abstract eternal MOTION, or its ensouling essence... Emanating from the one, eternal, abstract and purely quiescent Will (Âtmâ in Layam), it becomes Buddhi in its Alaya state, descends lower as Mahat (Manas) ... Will as an eternal principle is neither spirit nor substance but everlasting ideation."[1] HPB's definition prompts a question that goes to the core of our examination, which is this: What does it mean for this "will," as it exists in the human being, to be "free" when HPB asserts the prime characteristics of will are that (i) it governs the manifested universes, (ii) it is the ensouling essence of eternal motion, (iii) it emanates and descends through *ātmā-buddhi-manas* and further "down the ladder of degrees," and (iv) as an "eternal" principle it is neither spirit nor substance but eternal ideation? Certainly part of what it means is that will bears an inseparable relation to *ātmā-buddhi-manas* or the Inner Person, a principle not to be found as part of any discussion by modern secularists about free will, but which forms the basis of its definition and understanding according to the ancient wisdom tradition.

Much complexity, confusion and "white noise" can be productively eliminated from the inquiry into free will in light of the higher spiritual path by understanding the attributes and role of *choice*. In the literature on the question of free will among modern secularists, one is often confronted by "choice" and "free will" as more or less interchangeable terms. It should be acknowledged that this interchangeability can make sense within a narrow secular-rational context, where one is confined to quantitative and empirical strata of human activity that are navigable by reason, and where reference to the higher Self (*ātmā-buddhi-manas*) has been precluded from the discussion.

However, where the inquiry into free will is comprehensive—where it includes the traditional doctrine of the two selves—the discussion necessarily requires inclusion of a spectrum of the significance or *consequentiality* of choices one makes, as it were, from daily and ordinary and insignificant "micro-choices," to life-altering or "macro-choices." This latter includes *the* choice ultimately faced by the wayfarer on the higher spiritual journey to abandon fully the ways of the Outer Person in favor of following an initiatic path by centering his or her consciousness primarily within and through the Inner Person, regardless of whether he or she is currently under the tutelage of a qualified *guru*.

The level of choice we have referred to as "micro-choices" is an inextricable part of human life, whether we speak of the incarnate life of a human monad at the very beginning of its journey through human existence, or whether we speak of the incarnate life of an Adept such as Morya or KH effectively at the end of that journey. Micro-choices are those with little if any consequence as that pertains to the law of compensation, or mediate causes, commonly referred to as karma. Should I, on my way to my destination, walk in the sun or in the shade of the trees? Should I bypass the small fallen branch ahead, or step over it? Should I take my meal on the hour, or fifteen minutes later? Which pair of socks should I wear today? And so on with a myriad of such micro-choices, *ad infinitum*, which we as human beings often make every minute of the day in our ordinary and mundane activities.

Micro-choices remain with us throughout our spiritual journeys through human existence to the highest levels, as reflected in the statement by KH that "... an adept is an ordinary mortal at all moments of his daily life but those—when the *inner* man is acting."[2] Here is a good example of a spiritual model who acknowledges the truth of the doctrine of the two selves, where one is his mortal "ordinary" or Outer Man who acts as a "jailor" to his other immortal "Inner" Man. This realization points directly to the need of every Outer Person, even at the spiritually advanced level of KH, to make a series of micro-choices just to live through the ordinary days of a human being with all the material and subtle and often minor needs of existing in a physical body. Such a realization moves us closer to the traditional understanding of choice and free will in the context of the Inner Person (*ātmā-buddhi-manas*).

Summarizing our discussion of *choice*, we may say that wherever in modern, secularist discourse choice and free will are generally used interchangeably, it is predictable in that context to conclude that because human beings have choice at *any* level of significance — even micro-choices—they must therefore have free will. Thus, within this context, where one chooses to have orange juice rather than tangerine juice at the breakfast buffet, *this* choice becomes part of that corpus of secularist evidence that human beings are endowed with free will. And while in that secular context this conclusion covers everything from mundane and inconsequential micro-choices to providential life-altering macro-choices that may even include forfeiture of one's own life, for example, this conclusion that free will is equivalent to choice can be *reasoned* no further and halts at the portal of intuition (*buddhi*). Intuition, being an indispensable faculty for perception through the higher Self, allows the wayfarer to align his or her consequential choices through the *manas* while being guided by the emanating will of that higher spiritual state of *ātmā-buddhi-manas*—a form of choice beyond the reach of that cognition preferred by the secularists.

If one were to research the written philosophic legacy of free will in Latin and certain other European languages beginning around the time of the "Enlightenment" in Europe (*ca.* mid-17th century) to the present, one would find a sizeable volume of material identifiable as secular and based solely in reason. There are, in fact, contemporary academic specialists in free will who have both gathered past sources and presented original contributions on this topic, a growing area of interest in philosophy within academia. One such was the late Professor Michael Frede of Oxford University who published *A Free Will: Origins of the Notion in Ancient Thought*.[3]

In the classrooms and literature of modern, secularist academia where contributions are made to this inquiry in the books of its publishing houses and papers appearing in pedagogical journals of philosophy, one finds the precepts of free will and "fate"—in the form of fatalism, or alternatively "causal determinism," and their derivatives—juxtaposed as opposing propositions. Ironically, there is also a juxtaposition of free will and fate in the esotericist perspective, though it bears no resemblance to its secularist counterpart. In this perennial philosophy, which contains the doctrine of the two selves, fate may be said to apply only the Outer Person, whose mortal existence must inevitably suffer a "fatal" end, while free will applies to the Inner, and immortal, Person.

In stark opposition to this perspective is that of the secularist, whose analyses are typically limited to the Outer Person, and whose competing ideas are that the mortal person either (i) has unconditioned free will and thus is able to make true choices by suffering their consequences, or (ii) does *not* have free will—all such putative "choices" being conditioned by having been predetermined either from the cumulative prior actions of the person, or alternatively by a divine Creator. While in the secularist perspective fatalism and determinism—and their other derivative "isms"—may differ in significant ways, they share in common the characteristic that they are both set in opposition to free will, and pertain exclusively to the Outer Person. And within secularist philosophical discourse, this opposition invariably devolves into polemical disputes whose proffered premises and arguments—and fallacies—grow ever more impenetrable and are, at least for the esotericist, wholly unsatisfying as it relates to a clear understanding of free will.

One should not conclude from this that the esotericist perspective of free will is simple to understand—it is not. It is, however, at least simpler to understand than the various competing secularist philosophical views of free will, and that because there is only one way—rather than multiple ways—of perceiving it within the context of the *philosophia perennis*. And that one way is predicated on the ability that the wayfarer who seeks to understand has developed his or her higher reason and intuition in such a way that they operate, and apprehend, together.

The esotericist view of free will rests in the acknowledgment and understanding of the principle of the two selves, and was skillfully articulated by Ananda Coomaraswamy, who wrote that "Our sense of free will is as valid in itself as our sense of being, and as invalid as our sense of being So-and-so [Outer Person]. There *is* a free will, a will, that is, unconstrained by anything external to its own nature; but it is only 'ours' to the extent that we have abandoned all that we mean in common sense by 'ourselves' and our 'own' willing. Only *His* [Inner Person] service is perfect freedom."[4] This traditional conception of free will does not, to repeat, mean that those who act by and through the Inner Person are exempt from having any choices at all, or exempt from making decisions. Where micro-choices and decisions are linked to the contingent and material needs of living incarnate in a body, whether an ordinary individual or an initiated *jivanmukta*, one will yet have a panoply of inconsequential and everyday choices concerning the minutiae of ordinary activities.

Earlier we addressed micro- and macro-choices, and this precept denotes the critical difference between the type of choices referred to just above as those that are inescapable simply by virtue of existing in a physical body, and the type of momentous choice that involves which of the two selves shall predominate in one's incarnate existence. In the content of classic treatises and scriptures of the ancient wisdom tradition, Coomarasway noted that "... the natures and character of the two selves are treated at great length, and the importance of the resolution of their inner conflict emphasized; no man being at peace with himself until an agreement has been reached as to *which shall rule*" (emphasis added).[5] Which "self" shall rule thus becomes *the* predicate macro-choice.

This "inner conflict" between the two selves to which Coomaraswamy refers is nothing less than that which *must* at some point generate the life-altering choice, the decision, of which initial direction one seeks to take as between (i) a normal, ordinary existence or (ii) ascending the higher spiritual path. One alternative is to remain subject to the vicissitudes if not the tyranny of the Outer Person, even where one generally lives a "good" life. Because it is controlled by fate and the corresponding forces of appetite, desire, and attachment, the alternative of choosing the Outer Person as one's "ruler" is that of continued death and rebirth, and so is necessarily always fatal, *i.e.*, subject to Fate. Not only is this alternative fatal, but it is often described in the perennial philosophy as the way of bondage, where the Outer Person has imprisoned the Inner and acts as its jailor, and which therefore creates a situation wherein true free will does not, or more accurately cannot, apply.

The other alternative is living and being within the Inner Person, the way of everlasting liberation from that fatal cycle, and in ever greater degrees synchronizing or joining one's will to the Universal or cosmic will, whose end result is *complete* free will. At a higher level, this momentous decision—choosing between these two directions—is memorialized in the sacred treatises and scriptures of time, such as HPB's *The Voice of the Silence*. Where this choice is rightly made, it is fundamentally baptismal if not initiatic—a dramatic ascent from corruptible mortality to incorruptible immortality. It is the same macro-choice between "glory or gloom" once expressed by Mabel Collins: "Each man is his own absolute lawgiver, the dispenser of glory or gloom to himself; the decreer of his life, his reward, his punishment..."[6]

A renown illustration of such a choice is the mythic parable of Hiram Abiff, in the Masonic tradition, the "widow's son" who chose to face death rather than to divulge Masonic secrets he had sworn to keep. After being murdered in the Temple by three ruffians demanding these secrets from him, whom he steadfastly refused, Hiram Abiff was resurrected to a new and wholly spiritual life by his Master. This sacrificial motif is repeated in a number of the world's mythologies and scriptures in the form of heroic rebirth, or resurrection, as ably described by Mircea Eliade in *Rites and Symbols of Initiation: The Mysteries of Birth and Rebirth*.[7]

This macro-choice motif can be represented in a corresponding principle as choosing between chaos and cosmos, between darkness and light, and between the profane and the sacred, among others. But it can also be expressed as a choice between (i) *preserving* the status quo of one's familiar spiritual path and continuing to make gradual progress in terms of selflessness and other related qualities needed for eventual admission to probation as a prospective *chela* of an Adept in the Order whose members form the spiritual hierarchy of humanity; or (ii) *acting* on the conviction that one is ready for such admission and leaving behind everything familiar and comfortable, plunging headlong without equivocation into the quest for probation and chelaship under an Adept to whom one perceives a connection.

Accordingly, in the *philosophia perennis* free will occurs, without further terminological complexity or confusion, where the successful wayfarer chooses the latter course and is thereafter able by the guidance of his or her *guru* to synchronize the individual will operating through the Inner Person (*ātmā-buddhi-manas*) to the Universal or cosmic will. When this finally occurs, the wayfarer is no longer faced with any *consequential* or macro- "choices" between "... two or more alternative courses of action; at that point one knows that there is only one right thing to do and it becomes a question of whether one has the requisite ability [*i.e.*, will] to do it."[8] This is the essence of true "free will" in the esoteric tradition, being a sacredly symbiotic condition to which Coomaraswamy referred when he wrote that "In this [perennial] philosophy we are unfree to the extent that our willing is determined by the desires of the outer man, and free to the extent that the outer man has learnt to act, not for himself, but as the agent of the inner man, our real Self."[9]

8

Love & Hatred on the Higher Spiritual Path

In the silence of love you will find the spark of life.
– Jalal al-Din Rumi

Before engaging in any meaningful discussion of love and hatred from the standpoint of the *philosophia perennis*, one must first review the principle of *polarity* which, as a first principle within this primordial philosophy, is both immutable and immemorial. This review is necessary because love and hatred represent the "two poles of man's 'Soul,'" as the Adept KH stated, expressly identifying them as a classic example of the binary nature of polarity. Understood as feelings, or emotions, by initiates of the Order of which the Adepts Morya and KH are members, love and hatred are more particularly described by KH as *"immortal feelings."* As such, together these two immortal feelings are both unique and an exception to the rule that all those related components of feeling comprising this 4th of the seven principles of the human being—the *kamarupa* or the seat of emotion—disintegrate at some point after death, in the transition from death to rebirth. The significance of this relatively obscure exception for the wayfarer on the higher spiritual path cannot be overstated. The choices he or she makes based upon strong emotion that implicate love or hatred as the two opposite poles of this axis, and including their varying degrees on the active axis between these poles, will necessarily have both immediate and lasting effects on the wayfarer's higher spiritual journey.

Polarity, which is effectively synonymous with duality, and the ultimate *synthesis* of its two opposite poles into a unity or oneness, is a core pillar among the first principles of the ancient wisdom tradition. In the Vedas, for example, this principle is expressed by the concepts of *purusha* and *prakriti*. The former is the active or masculine principle, while the latter is the passive or feminine principle, which represent two axial poles of all manifestation in the universe. In the Vedānta, this principle of duality is expressed by the term *dvaita*, whose synthesis is *advaita*. Other ancient, sacred scriptures and associated historical literature similarly abound in references to this principle, the most visible of which are found in the Taoist (yin/yang), Buddhist tantric (*yab-yum*), and Hellenistic Gnostic[1] expressions. Polarity, as a principle, is also recognized in various forms in most major religious traditions. In addition, this principle was a key element of pre-Socratic thought, evidenced by the "table of [ten] opposites" formulated by Pythagoras, and later preserved by way of Aristotle in his *Metaphysics*. All these writings, collectively, assert that the first principle of polarity—and concomitantly the *coincidentia oppositorum* (the synthesis or "co-incidence of opposites")—can be found at every level of manifestation and in every manifested modality or operation up to that transformative point of co-incidence.

HPB often addressed the principle of polarity, or contraries, or opposites, in reference to various phenomena. Among her most succinct statements, and one that illustrates a correspondence of the macro-principle with the micro-subject, is the following:

Esoteric philosophy admits neither good nor evil *per se*, as existing independently in nature. The cause for both is found, as regards the Kosmos, in the necessity of contraries or contrasts, and with respect to man, in his human nature, his ignorance and passions. There is no *devil* or the utterly depraved, as there are no Angels absolutely perfect, though there may be spirits of Light and Darkness; thus Lucifer... is the Logos in his highest, and the "adversary" in his lowest—both of which are reflected in our *Ego*.[2]

Perhaps most important is this human perspective where, as elsewhere, these two opposites are in a constant state of flux or intercourse and tension, striving for resolution or reconciliation. This was emphasized by Thomas Aquinas in his formulation *duo sunt in homine* (literally, "two there are in man"), further illustrating the centrality of this principle as the "two selves" who dwell together in one human being. These two Inner/Higher and Outer/Lower contraries of the human being, just like the immortal feelings of love and hatred, are connected as correlatives. As HPB observed, these opposites or contraries always manifest as pairs, examples of which are light, selflessness and supra-consciousness on one pole, and darkness, selfishness, and unconsciousness on the other—none existing independently *per se*, but rather as interrelated yet polar contraries along the same axis. We may also add to these the moral concepts of good and evil.

What might be called the supreme aspect of polarity is its resolution or synthesis as duad-into-monad, occasionally rendered as *syzygy* from the Greek *suzugiā*, meaning "union." This resolution is the coincidence of opposites in which duality must, at some point, dissolve before and into the *one*, or absolute unity. This is the transmorphic act of the co-incidence of its binary nature, effectively equilibrizing and neutralizing itself in the process of uniting. This two-subsumed-in-one is not only the final goal of human endeavor, but also the *ens perfectissimum* of esoteric metaphysics. And in a practical sense it is, for the wayfarer, the achievement of total liberation—*moksa* of Hinduism and *nirvāna* of Buddhism—and reintegration with unconditioned Being. This aspect of polarity is, in short, among the most sublime and sacred themes of the *philosophia perennis*, of *theosophia*. It has been alluded to in the various religio-philosophical and esoteric or occult systems as full enlightenment, transformation, or God-realization—terms that may be peculiar to specific traditions or doctrines but which convey the same meaning. Stated most succinctly, it is complete synthesis or *coincidentia oppositorum*, each pole transubstantiated into the other, forming one of the two, or sublimating the duad into a unified, holistic, and unconditioned state beyond all contraries and conditions.

As exemplars of the principle of polarity, we learn from KH that "*Love* and *Hatred* are the only *immortal* feelings, the only survivors from the wreck of *Ye-dhamma*, or the phenomenal world."[3] We may safely extrapolate from this that love and hatred are survivors of the dissolution of the phenomenal world, which includes the "lower quaternary" or lower four of the seven principles of the human being. Accordingly, love and hatred, being *immortal* feelings and as such shielded as an exception to the rule that all lower phenomena of the human being must disintegrate after this "wreck" we call death, partially integrate with the noumenal world of the "higher triad" of these seven principles, being *ātmā* (7th principle), *buddhi* (6th principle), and *manas* (5th principle), during the transition from death to rebirth. These higher principles are the "spiritual faculties" of which KH speaks when he adds that "Out of the resurrected Past [prior incarnation] *nothing* remains but what the Ego has felt *spiritually*—that was evolved by and through, and lived over by his spiritual faculties—be they *love* or *hatred*."[4] It is significant that KH uses the verb form "felt" to explain the resurrection of love and hatred in the *post-mortem* state of *devachan*—and potentially in subsequent incarnations—in contrast to the non-emotional or purely intellectual "recollections" of one's prior spiritual milestones.

If the survival of the emotions of love and hatred is an *exception* to the rule that feelings or emotions, as progeny of the *kamarupa* (4th principle) in alliance with *manas rupa* (lower 5th principle), do not survive the transition from death to rebirth, what then is the full context of that rule? As discussed above in a previous essay, the rule is that upon one's death the lower three principles—the

1st or physical body, the 2nd or etheric body, and the 3rd or vital body (*jivatma*)—all die together at the moment of death, and thus separate from the remaining higher four principles that then exist together, temporarily, in the *kamaloka*. There follows a "death struggle" of the 7th and 6th principles versus the 5th and 4th principles and, where the higher two principles prevail, they attract to themselves "... the quintessence of *Good* from the fifth [principle] ... and the most Spiritualised portions of its mind [higher 5th principle]—follows its divine *elder* (the 7th) into the 'Gestation' state."[5] KH further adds to this that at the end of this death struggle "... the sixth and seventh [principles] carrying off a portion of the fifth [principle] ..." enter the gestation state with "... the spiritual spoil from the fifth [principle] ..."[6]

Significantly, with regard to the events of the *post-mortem* transition neither KH nor Morya provides any detail about the exception that emotions of love or hatred may be part of this "spoil" that survives the initial *post-mortem* states as a component of the immortal reincarnating entity of the human being—the spiritual Monad, or transmigrant. KH does explain, though, that no other feelings in the bliss of *devachan* exist "... outside that immortal feeling of love and sympathetic attraction whose seeds are planted in the fifth, whose plants blossom luxuriantly in and around the fourth, but whose roots have to penetrate deep into the sixth principle..."[7]

As the polar opposite to *devachan*, one is left to speculate whether this or a similar process may apply to hatred in that tragic *post-mortem* state called *avichi*, that KH once described as "the perfect antithesis of *devachan*." *Avichi* is the sorrowful destination for those who traveled the *via obscura* or dark path through their incarnations, and who were able to salvage no feelings "outside that immortal feeling" of hatred. These pitiable beings who were driven in their lives almost exclusively by greed, selfishness, envy, fear, predation, dishonesty, and extortion or control of others eventually suffer a complete break or separation of their lower principles from their highest spiritual principles, due to the weight of the oppositive karma arising from this way of life. Though in *avichi* their subsequent fates may vary depending on a variety of factors, these fates usually share in common aeons of misery and suffering until, in most cases, their ultimate annihilation as evolving beings occasioned by the departure of the overshadowing *buddhi* and *ātmā* to their sources. The reader is advised that while this subject should form part of a thorough intellectual study of the course of humanity in its spiritual evolution, as a principle the darkness and devolution of *avichi* comprises the antithesis of the contents and purpose of these essays, and for this reason no more about it shall be said.

For the wayfarer on the higher spiritual path, the significance of the immortality of the emotion of love and its survival into *devachan*, and potentially from one incarnation to another, should be immediately obvious. As regards the cartage of the essence of immortal love and hatred by the transmigrant into future incarnations, we learn from Morya that "Man has his seven principles, the germs of which he brings with him at his birth."[8] Imbedded, therefore, in the "spoil" of the 5th principle that forms part of the reincarnating Monad of each human being, immortal love or hatred arguably can return in new incarnations within the "germs" of which Morya speaks. Along the axis of love and hatred, where the wayfarer makes consequential life decisions while not yet having reached a condition of *true* free will, their spiritual consequences may be either salvational or catastrophic.

Given that love and hatred are the extreme poles of an axis, we must acknowledge that a wide space exists along this axis where these opposite emotions begin to merge and even overlap, not unlike brackish water formed by the confluence where the fresh waters of large rivers meet the saltwater of the sea. As KH writes,

Yes; *Love* and *Hatred* are the only immortal feelings; but the gradations of tones along the seven by seven scales of the whole key-board of life, are numberless. And, since it is those two feelings—(or... those two poles of man's "Soul" which is a unity)—that mould the future state of man, whether for *Devachan* or *Avitchi* then the variety of such states must also be inexhaustible.[9]

It is seldom if ever that one is faced with a choice between pure or absolute love, and pure or absolute hatred. As KH points out, "the gradations of tones" along the length of the active axis in between the polar extremes of love and hatred are "numberless." Such choices, then, are almost always more subtle than stark, and often more ambiguous than clear. Where circumstances are ambiguous, it may not always be easy to discern selfless intent from selfish intent when confronted with life choices. In short, wayfarers and probationers may have "mixed emotions" when confronting such issues in their daily lives.

The principal challenge for the wayfarer treading the higher spiritual path, therefore, is to be able to discern accurately among ambiguous love-hate emotions when making significant life choices, and similarly to avoid developing an indifference or apathy that ignores love. For the wayfarer who is fortunate enough to have achieved a state of genuine free will, these choices are effectively made with and for him or her by the omniscience of that synthesis with universal or cosmic will. *Free* will occurs only where the wayfarer has been able to sufficiently *synchronize* his or her individual will operating through the Inner Person (*ātmā-buddhi-manas*) to the universal or cosmic will. However, where that higher state has not yet been fully achieved, and the choices to be made lie within this brackish maze or "the gradations of tones" between the poles of love and hatred, the consequences of making the correct—or incorrect—choice are profound. Committing oneself completely and consistently to the way of universal love, for example, in the life choices one makes within this axis of love and hatred, is to love well and thereby to receive its rewards. This idea is reflected in the words of KH, who wrote that "Unless a man *loves* well or *hates* as well, he will be neither in Devachan nor in Avitchi"[10] during the *post-mortem* transition.

In their writings a fair amount of attention is paid by the Adepts Moyra and KH, and by HPB, to the *via obscura*, the path of darkness where fear and hatred and lust for power flourish as methods, if not goals. At one point KH refers to "... the two kinds of the initiates—the adepts and the sorcerers,"[11] also referring to the latter as "Brethren of the Shadow." Among the varying groups worldwide whose members practice these "dark arts" is a discrete order of Himalayan cenobites known as *dugpas*, with whom Morya and KH and those of their Order were most familiar. Further, we learn from KH that these brethren of the Shadow also have "rules" in their orders, and train neophytes in their insidious methods of operation which include seduction and extortion, among others, in order to gain complete control of their victims. Rather than seeking to exert control over oneself for the benefit of others, as do the Adepts and their *chelas*, the sorcerers seek to exert control and power over others for their own selfish ends, following the "left hand" or pole of polarity among whose elements are selfishness and evil, and where hatred is utilized as an emotion of destructive force. As HPB noted, "Very luckily few outside the high practitioners of the Left Path and of the Adepts of the Right... understand the 'black' [magic] evocations... [and that] sorcerers hate all those who are not with them, arguing that, therefore, they are against them."[12] The consequences of choosing this path of darkness are ultimately isolation and annihilation as a human transmigrant, and the entry into *avichi* can be relatively proximate in the being's entire cycle of transmigration.

In fact, it should not be surprising that Morya, KH, and HPB make reference to this *via obscura* throughout their writings, even while expressly promoting the *via lucis*, the "path of light" for those whose goal is further spiritual advancement. This is so because, first, the *via obscura* represents the polar opposite of the chosen paths of these Adepts. It thus provides a stark counterpoint for choosing between these two paths, under the precept that things are largely defined by their opposites. But second, and more importantly, probationers and even newly accepted *chelas* remain at risk, for example, by becoming intoxicated with new powers they may have developed or by succumbing to selfish urges of a swollen personal ego, and possibly sliding backwards into that other path. There are no guarantees when the wayfarer's spiritual quest reaches these levels, *even* under the watchful eye of the *guru*, since we are each the navigator on our own journey, and each our "own absolute lawgiver, the dispenser of glory or gloom" to ourselves. The temptations are both strong and dangerous and, as Morya once wrote to his *chela* Ramaswami Iyer, even "An accepted chela does not become free from temptation, probations, and trials."[13]

Nonetheless, the fact remains that the sphere of the *via obscura* harbors the emotion of hatred, while the sphere of the *via lucis* harbors the emotion of love, and that each is the polar opposite of the other. For the wayfarer on the higher spiritual path it is also crucial to distinguish, in any discussion of love, differences in that emotion which can be more clearly understood by early Greek terms. The Greeks developed several separate terms under the rubric of love, but for our purposes we need focus only on two. These are *érōs*—from which the English word "erotic" derives—having mostly to do with a personal and specific love, and *agápe*, having mostly to do with an impersonal and unconditional love, as the Adepts and their *chelas* have for humanity as a whole. Accordingly, it is only that love, *agápe*, of which we speak in this discussion. This is the love needed to tread the higher spiritual path, as noted by KH when he wrote that he was "... not only taught, but desirous to subordinate every preference for individuals to a love for the human race."[14] This is the love of all beings and compassion for their suffering. It is the Buddhist ideal of the *bodhisattva* whose adherents practice *metta*, translated from the Pāli as "loving kindness," and for whom "Compassion is no attribute. It is the LAW OF LAWS—eternal Harmony Ālaya's SELF; a shoreless universal essence, the light of everlasting Right, and fitness of all things, the law of love eternal."[15]

At this point in humanity's cycle of duration, the ominous shadow of the *via obscura* appears to be steadily advancing upon our globe in numerous forms, including political autocracy, injustice, aggression, disinformation, and extreme natural disasters from climate change. For this reason, a continuous effort must be made to promote its opposite—the *via lucis*— as an antidote to the despair and suffering that follow in the wake of these dark forces. Those who consider themselves to be wayfarers on the higher spiritual path must then respond without equivocation by following the religion of the heart and choosing love as their path, and so *radiating* love since, as HPB ably notes, "Hatred is never quenched by hatred; hatred ceases by showing love; this is an old rule."[16] And this "old rule," as HPB says, is the key to equilibrizing and neutralizing the effects of hatred and darkness so apparent in the world's affairs and conditions. One cannot travel the two opposite paths simultaneously: one must choose a path and follow it until a final point of synthesis is reached. These dark forces can only be neutralized by radiating universal and unconditional love up to that mystic point of coincidence of darkness and light, of hatred and love, when the wayfarer at last escapes the limitations and constraints of the pairs of opposites, of contraries, and finally of all conditions, and ascends to the ineffable state of synthesis and unconditioned oneness beyond them. But this "escape" does not mean that this wayfarer ceases to be involved with the needs of humanity. In fact, just the reverse is true, since where the wayfarer has followed the path of the *bodhisattva*, his or her new and sole objective is to relieve the suffering of humanity by helping to lead it to spiritual enlightenment.

But until that ineffable state is reached, a sustained effort by the wayfarer on the path of light consciously to radiate and project loving kindness, the "immortal feeling," to all people, to all sentient beings, is necessary to offset the pall of global angst, fear and suffering. Just as our mentors the Adepts do, it should become part of the wayfarer's duty to project and broadcast through all available media the hope and consolation that inheres in the path of love and light. By example, he or she should be a constant reminder to others that the reality of love is the breathtaking and shimmering beauty of prismatic emanations radiating from the *ātmā* and *buddhi*. This radiance includes the calm and spiritually luminous brilliance that "embraces all in oneness," the welcome solace of warmth that simulates the rays of the sun which nurture and bless everything they touch, unconditionally and indiscriminately. All this is spiritual beauty of love, and contained in what is meant by "divine pulchritude."

And together with this beauty will the immortal feeling of love for humanity accompany the wayfarer into *devachan* for a time, and possibly into future incarnations, and amplify his or her role as a spiritual being. This is because, as the Adept Morya observed, "It is he alone who has the love of humanity at heart, who is capable of grasping thoroughly the idea of a regenerating practical Brotherhood, who is entitled to the possession of our secrets."[17]

9

The Providential Higher Spiritual Path

It is much rather Fate (the operation of mediate causes, karma)
that "allots" or "provides for" the being of things as they are, than
Providence, which is the timeless witness of this operation.
– Ananda K. Coomaraswamy

The English word "providence," and its adjectival form
"providential," both stem from the verb "to provide." While this
noun and adjective are used in multiple ways in literature of the
English-speaking world, in theological discourse "Providence"
has a special meaning. In particular, Providence or one of its
synonyms appears regularly in religions that do *not* have a
developed doctrine based on the principle which in Sanskrit is
rendered *karma*. In those religions—especially the Abrahamic
religions of Judaism, Christianity, and Islam—providence is
generally understood as the preordained plan of the one God,
or through this plan what God *provides* to each and every
person, to all humankind collectively, and to the planet with all
its creatures and features. Under this doctrine, whatever benign
or malign occurrence befalls an individual is due to or the result
of this preordained plan—it is the outcome of Providence.

For many devout adherents of exoteric religions, the cosmic
scheme of divine Providence is essentially one of intellectual
security or comfort. This because it allows all phenomena
and events on our terrestrial plane—however unfair or
random or inscrutable they may seem—to be fully and easily
explained and rationalized simply as God's will. But for
those wayfarers who tread the rigorous higher spiritual path
of probation and chelaship under an Adept, or who hope to,
the relevance of providence is more immediate and profound.

"Divine Providence" of organized religions may be viewed as a construct—a theological apotropaic to ward off uncertainty and angst. But providence for wayfarers on the higher spiritual path is actual and real, and often manifests as opportunities and protections provided to *chelas* by their *gurus*. The difference between these two forms of providence, and the precise operation of that between Adept and *chela*, is the subject we shall explore in this essay.

Within the exoteric framework of the Abrahamic religions, Providence is both a central belief and one that applies to everyone who shares the theological notions that all of humankind are children of the one God who, as their Father, is protector and provider. Moses Mendelssohn, among the greatest Jewish thinkers of the Enlightenment, wrote that "Essentially, the religion of the Israelites encompasses only three central principles: God, Providence, and legislation."[1] In Christianity, while the term Providence is not found in the scriptures *per se*, thus allowing a conclusion that it is more a dogmatic than a strictly theological precept, Providence is nonetheless thoroughly infused in the New Testament and its pastoral exegesis. The meaning of *Matthew* 10:29-30 is clear: "Are not two sparrows sold for a penny? And not one of them will fall to the ground without your Father's will. But even the hairs of your head are all numbered." And in Islam, the idea of Providence (*kismat*) is so central to its doctrine that it occurs in a universal and frequent expression of conversational speech as "*inshā'Allāh*," being Arabic for "God willing" and predicated upon preordination and the belief that nothing happens unless God has willed it.

In what may at first appear as a contradistinction to the Providence of the Abrahamic religions stand the religions of Hinduism and Buddhism, whose views of the provision of all things are ultimately based in the law of *karma*. In these Eastern religions, most adherents accept that whatever benign or malign occurrence befalls an individual is the result of his or her past actions (*karma*) in this or in previous lives, and not due to the automation of a preordained deific plan. Omitting momentarily the Adept-to-*chela* analysis that will be discussed shortly, HPB conveyed dual perspectives of Providence in her writings—unfavorable and favorable, respectively. However, her perspective on the karmic doctrine was constant, and her insightful contrasts and comparison of *karma* to Providence help resolve their apparent contradistinction.

HPB was usually unequivocal in her distaste for the reliance of those of the Abrahamic religions—Christian clerics mostly being the subject of her disfavor—on the concept of Providence as God's preordained plan. Speaking of Christian clergymen generally, she wrote that "The clergy, by teaching the helplessness of man, his utter dependence on Providence, and the doctrine of atonement, have crushed in their faithful followers every atom of self-reliance and self-respect."[2] While this statement speaks of some *results* of mindless reliance on divine Providence, through several specific complaints HPB explained what she believed ultimately generated this errant concept of Providence leading to such reliance, or "dependence" to use her term.

HPB's first such complaint regarding reliance on the notion of Providence was that it is too easy an excuse—or worse, a sacerdotal prohibition—for avoiding any meaningful inquiry into the universal laws of nature and the powers latent in human beings. With few exceptions, she believed that virtually all of nature and the universe could be comprehended and understood by human beings as they progressed spiritually, were introduced to the ancient wisdom or *theosophia*, and began to access divine Intellect. She complained that "God being intelligence itself, and the soul his agent likewise intelligent. Whence the imperfection, the evil, the failures of nature? Who is responsible for all this? Or shall we be answered by Christian occultists as we have hitherto been by their orthodox brethren: 'the ways of Providence are mysterious and it is a sin to question them'?"[3]

Another of HPB's complaints about the dependence on Providence by the devout was that it is often generated by "sentimentality" and "human conceit." This latter was a reference she made to an intellectual conceit that believes humans capable of constructing a cogent thesis of purpose or meaning that both ignores and conflicts with a core law of the universe—the law of compensation. In addressing one of her correspondents who invoked divine Providence to explain such "miraculous" events as apparently inexplicable survivals of one or two individuals in mass tragedies, HPB bluntly asks "... why is it, that to every such *one* case of *miraculous* escape, there are 10,000 cases where human beings are left to perish brutally and stupidly without any seeming fault on their part, their death being often the starting point of the most disastrous subsequent results, and this with no providence, no spirit interfering to stop the merciless hand of blind fate?" She answers her own question: "It is pure sentimentality alone, with selfish pride and human conceit to help it, that can evolve such theories to account for every exceptional occurrence."[4] HPB forcefully adds that "*Karma*, and our inner, unconscious (so far as our physical senses go) prevision can alone explain such cases of unexpected escapes."

Further, HPB objected to the metaphysical error of divine Providence as an explanation or reason for various inventions and advances in science, and the hypocrisy it instigated when used by clergymen. In support of her objection, she cited published criticisms by clerics, for example, to railroads because God did not intend for human beings to travel at such speeds; to the advent of telegraphs as the "tempting of Providence"; and to the introduction of anesthetics for women in childbirth. This last objection sorely irritated HPB, given one theologian's stated rationale that these anesthetics were "an impious attempt to escape from the curse denounced against all women in *Genesis*, iii, 16." She immediately added: "... those same Bishops do not hesitate to meddle with the work of Providence when the 'heathen' are concerned. Surely if Providence hath so decreed that women should be left to suffer for the sin of Eve, then it must have also willed that a man, born a heathen should be left one as—preordained."[5]

There was, however, another side of HPB's utilization of the term providence that might be called favorable, and it contained both neutral and positive usage of the term. HPB would occasionally abandon her disfavor of the term and use it in a neutral sense, as in the following:

> You will observe that, in this is contained the transition from the Infinite to the Finite... the proceeding of Heterogeneity from Homogeneity or Multifariousness from Unity—of matter or form from pure Intelligence or Principle without form—the operation of pure intelligence upon matter, and this in spite of the infinite *gulf* between them—the relationship of Creator to Creature or Creations, so as to be able to exercise supervision on what we call Providence or law, or Order.[6]

In this "neutral" usage above, HPB comes close to making providence synonymous with the "law or order" of *karma*. In this regard, we also find that HPB ventured at times from her unfavorable usage of the word providence by affirmatively aligning it—favorably—with the Greek goddess Nemesis. This alignment is significant because it can be described as HPB's positive usage of the term providence, at least when *combined* with the powers of Nemesis. The daughter of Nyx and Erebus (sometimes Oceanus), Nemesis was the mythic goddess of divine retribution, alternately referred to as the goddess of proportion, and poetically described as the "daughter of Justice." Her name derives from the Greek word *némein*, meaning "to give what is due."

"In short," HPB wrote, "while Nemesis is a mythological, exoteric goddess, or *Power*, personified and anthropomorphized in its various aspects, *Karma* is a highly philosophical truth, a most divine noble expression of the primitive intuition of man concerning Deity."[7] But notwithstanding these differences of retributive "power" and "truth," HPB nonetheless aligns Nemesis here with *karma*. This alignment is brought to crystal clarity in another express statement by HPB on Nemesis and *karma*:

> Karma-Nemesis is the synonym of PROVIDENCE, minus *design*, goodness, and every other *finite* attribute and qualification, so unphilosophically attributed to the latter. An Occultist or a philosopher will not speak of the goodness or cruelty of Providence; but, identifying it with Karma-Nemesis, he will teach that nevertheless it guards the good and watches over them in this, as in future lives; and that it punishes the evil-doer—aye, even to his seventh rebirth... For the only decree of Karma—an eternal and immutable decree—is absolute Harmony in the world of matter as it is in the world of Spirit.[8]

With this grudging allowance of providence, as personified by Nemesis and synonymized with *karma*, we are finally able to discern HPB's dichotomous and somewhat complicated perception of the term. There is, however, little evidence in their writings that HPB's teachers, the Adepts, shared the same antipathy for the term providence, or even had ambivalent views of the term, which we can glean from the infrequent—compared to HPB—appearance the term has in their writings. The Adept KH, for example, wrote that "If you ask a learned

Buddhist priest, what is Karma?—he will tell you that Karma is what a Christian might call Providence (in a certain sense only) and a Mahomedan—*Kismet,* fate or destiny (again in one sense)."[9]

The same matter-of-fact use of providence is also found in a letter from the Adept Serapis Bey to Henry Olcott, in which this Adept refers to HPB—in pointed though unintended irony—as herself a "providence." He tells Olcott in a remarkably prescient statement that "Her [HPB's] letter to thee and thy own knowledge of human heart must inspire thee, O Brother, with the words best adapted for this plan... how dangerous for her will be the achievement of her duty and how likely to expect for both of you to lose a sister and a—Providence on earth."[10] Olcott did in fact lose his "sister" HPB in 1891, whom he outlived by sixteen years until his death in 1907. And those who truly appreciate the extraordinary work HPB did for humanity, and the awful sacrifices she endured to do so, can also fully appreciate what the Adept declared—that HPB was *herself* a providence, providing to us in clear modern English comprehensive and outstanding restatements of the immemorial truths of the *philosophia perennis.*

"For the Occultist," wrote HPB, "this enigma of the [apparent] unequal favor of Karma or Providence is unriddled by the Secret Doctrine."[11] This terse quote observes a profound truth that is meaningful on several levels. With this quote HPB introduces a principle that KH explains in greater detail. Regarding the providential nature of their work, KH asks, and answers:

How could your world collect proofs of the doings of men [Adepts] who have sedulously kept closed every possible door of approach by which the inquisitive could spy upon them? ... What they have done they know; all those outside their circle could perceive was results, the causes of which were masked from view. To account for these results, men have in different ages invented theories of the interposition of "Gods," Special providences, fates, and the benign or hostile influences of the stars. There never was a time within or before the so-called historical period when our [Adept] predecessors were not moulding events and "making history," the facts of which were subsequently and invariably distorted by "historians" to suit contemporary prejudices.[12]

It is clear from this statement that within the global realm of providence, the Adepts play a larger, more universal role than most realize. However, our purpose here is not to explore this universal role of providence or oversight of humanity that the Adepts undertake, but rather what specific oversight, or providence, the Adepts employ for the benefit of their *chelas*.

Before any *chela* can benefit from the instruction or providence of an Adept as his or her *guru*, that *chela* must effectively "leave home," wherein most needs of the *chela* had been met. This ancient principle, found in both Buddhism and Hinduism, has both a gradual and immediate application. In Buddhism, a "home-leaver" is similar to a "stream-enterer": one who abandons the mundane world and actively enters the stream that flows to release (*vimutti*) from the wheel of death and rebirth. Among the best paradigms of a home-leaver is found in the *Shōbōgenzō*, the massive work of the 13th-century Zen master Dogen who devoted an entire chapter to *Shukke* ("On Leaving Home Life Behind"). In Hinduism, a corresponding principle is found in *sannyasa*, the fourth of the "*ashramas*," from the Aśrama Upanishad. In this stage of life, the *sannyasi* sets out alone with alms bowl in hand, without any belongings, with no home or family, and with no real destination other than to seek final truth and possibly the attainment of liberation.

For the traditional Buddhist or Hindu devotee, these are choices that rely *entirely* on the dictates of *karma*-Nemesis as providence. In this context, to leave home is to leap into free-fall, where whether one's needs will be met is unknown. Virtually the same can be said for the wayfarer who seeks to become a probationer or especially a *chela* under an Adept of the Order to which Mörya, KH, Serapis Bey, and others belong. In that endeavor, *karma* is always the overriding context within which their providence occurs. KH asserted that "Since every one of us is the *creator* and producer of the *causes* that lead to such or some other *results*, we have to reap but what we have sown." That said, KH added: *"Our chelas are helped but when they are innocent of the causes that lead them into trouble;* when such causes are generated by foreign, outside influences."[13]

This type of help would normally apply to senior *chelas* like Djual Khul, and to junior *chelas* like Damodar Mavalankar, both of whom were "accepted" and had in fact "left home" in the physical or immediate sense,[14] and went to live in the Himalayas under the direct tutelage of the Adepts. However, this type of help would not normally apply to probationers, given KH's statement that until a *chela* "… has passed that period [probation], we leave him to fight out his battles as best he may; and have to do so occasionally with higher and *initiated* chelas such as H.P.B., once they are allowed to work in the world, that all of us more or less avoid."[15]

Authentic wayfarers on the higher spiritual path are typically in the process of leaving home. This often begins as an incremental dissociation from those practices and associations that bind them—as attachments—to their mundane lives, and so hinder their advanced spiritual progress. Once they arrive at the precincts of chelaship, these are they for whom KH wrote: "You will always get what you need as you shall deserve them [instructions], but no more than you deserve or are able to assimilate."[16] Such instructions, which are also a manifestation of providence, are accessible to wayfarers whose 6th principle (*buddhi*) has acquired the necessary resonance to apprehend them.

"Let those who really desire to learn *abandon all* and come to us, instead of asking or expecting us to go to them."[17] So wrote KH, consistent with the venerable principle of the need for wayfarers on the higher spiritual path to leave home—to choose to abandon all, to labor full time for the spiritual enlightenment of humanity. To achieve this wayfarers must have faith in both the Adepts and in the operation of *karma*-Nemesis that they, when necessary, will be provided for upon making this choice. This decision usually consists of personal and painful sacrifices, whether leaving home is incremental or all at once. The choice to abandon all and leave home, most often a departure from that which is familiar and comprises one's "comfort zone," is unsettling and at times frightening—a volitional dive into the unknown pertaining to the basics of emotional and even physical survival. But the guiding star is that this choice ultimately inures to the benefit of humanity, *especially* so in times of environmental crisis and global pandemics and political upheaval, and the fear and despair those events create, when the need for willing soldiers is so dire in the escalating global struggle between darkness and light.

KH advises all those considering this choice to believe that "You will not be unwatched and uncared for, but you have to attract not to repel us and our chelas."[18] Within the context of chelaship, to attract the attention of the Adepts is achieved only by being resolutely strong and fearless, and steadily living a life of intuition, selflessness, purity, and compassion. And after that attraction has been successful and Their powerful attention is directed at the new *chela*, being "watched and cared for" becomes the special providence of Adept to *chela*, alive in the words of Serapis Bey: "We keep watch over our faithful soldiers."[19]

10

Doubt & Conviction on the Higher Spiritual Path

*Our doubts are traitors, and make us lose the
good we oft might win, by fearing to attempt.*
– Shakespeare

After years or even lifetimes in the solemn and unremitting pursuit of spiritual truth, the serious seeker—the wayfarer—invariably reaches a point along the higher spiritual path which triggers the need to make one radical and life-altering decision. For such wayfarers this consequential decision—this choice—is typically one between two competing options. If chosen, either choice will affect directly the wayfarer's admission to probation as a prospective *chela* of an Adept in the brother/sister-hood of their ancient Order founded upon the principle of spiritual hierarchy. The first option is simply the preservation of *status quo* as that relates to continuing to follow one's familiar spiritual path by making gradual progress practicing routine spiritual disciplines like meditation and yoga together with some study of spiritual values, all the while living and working in the interactive and transient world not unlike most of one's neighbors.

The second option is choosing to *act* on the firm belief that one is ready to make a courageous though daunting ascent straight up the steep mountainside to the summit of spiritual truth, and so leave behind everything familiar and comfortable, plunging headlong without equivocation into the quest for probation and chelaship under an Adept to whom one perceives a connection. This latter choice was succinctly summarized by the Adept KH: "Let those who really desire to learn *abandon all* and come to us, instead of asking or expecting us to go to them."[1] It was KH who emphasized the words "abandon all" in his original letter.

Both these choices inevitably involve one of the five *kleśas* (Sanskrit for "obstacles" or "hindrances" in achieving *samādhi*) described in detail by Patañjali in his *Yoga Sutras*. The particular obstacle or *kleśa* that here draws our attention is known as *abhiniveśa*, and is translated as a desire to preserve or "cling to" the *status quo* of one's life. Those having chosen the second option to act, or launch forth in abandoning all, have overcome this powerful obstacle, while those who chose the first option continue to remain under its sway.

We are fortunate to have a reliable and detailed description, and analysis, of exactly such a consequential decision being made—in a single evening—by the attorney Henry S. Olcott, co-founder together with HPB of the Theosophical Society in the year 1875. This account is most useful in examining the question of doubt versus conviction on the higher spiritual path. Among the many other fascinating accounts and experiences of occult phenomena recorded by Olcott in his published six-volume memoir *Old Diary Leaves*, perhaps the most memorable is the account of Olcott's initial meeting with his *guru*, the Adept Morya. This unusual meeting took place in the final days of 1877 at the apartment in New York City that Olcott shared with his sister Isabella (known as Belle), and with HPB, which was dubbed the "Lamasery." Olcott records that after a long and tiring day, while he was alone in his room late one evening and relaxing in a chair reading,

All at once, as I read with my shoulder a little turned from the door, there came a gleam of something white in the right-hand corner of my right eye; I turned my head, dropped my book in astonishment, and saw towering above me in his great stature an Oriental clad in white garments... He was so grand a man, so imbued with the majesty of moral strength, so luminously spiritual, so evidently above average humanity, that I felt abashed in his presence, and bowed my head and bent my knee as one does before a god or god-like personage.[2]

Olcott devotes several pages of his published memoir to this remarkable event where his *guru*, an Adept then resident in the Himalayas, appeared through occult means and sat with him for some time, disclosing to him much about his future. As one result of this dramatic conversation, in which he also learned of his future in relation to that of HPB's with respect to their sacred mission in the world, Olcott further shares in his memoir his private thoughts and conclusions that were formed in the many years that followed this meeting until he wrote this account. Among other descriptions, Olcott relays that of all the numerous occult phenomena and experiences he witnessed throughout his life, this one "was the most momentous in its consequences upon the course of my life," and that "it was the chief among the causes of my abandoning of the world and coming out to my Indian home." Most significantly, as relates to our topic here, was his assertion that until this meeting occurred he could not see his way clear to "breaking the ties of circumstance" that "bound" him to America. He concluded further that unless it had occurred, he may have felt compelled to continuously postpone this difficult decision to a more "convenient season," as procrastinators tend to do. But, having in fact occurred, this extraordinary meeting with his *guru* settled his destiny, and "in an instant *doubts melted away* [emphasis added]" and "the clear foresight of a fixed will showed the way."[3]

The outcome of the entire event was effectively distilled by Olcott into a single sentence, which perfectly highlights the gaping chasm between doubt and conviction—conviction based on knowledge. Olcott declared as a result of this experience, as applied to both (i) the existence of the Adepts and (ii) whether the decision to abandon all and become a full-time *chela* was right, that "However others less fortunate may doubt, I KNOW."[4] The emphasis on the word "know" in this sentence is Olcott's.

Much can be drawn from Olcott's experience as it pertains to the proper state of mind needed for arriving at the decision to devote oneself fully both in thought and *deed* to the principle of the eternal, rather than continuing to apply a significant portion of one's energy to that which is impermanent and ephemeral. In making such a decision, it is perhaps more accurate to refer to one's "state of intuition" in collaboration with one's "state of mind," than solely to one's state of "mind." What is required to make such a decision wisely involves a collaboration of the higher 5th and 6th principles, *manas arupa* and *buddhi*, or that which comports with the better and higher capabilities of reason and intuition operating in tandem, if not in synthesis.

It may be tempting to draw from this single experience of Olcott a functional paradigm of the decision that all who aspire to ascend the higher reaches of the spiritual path must one day make: to decide and thus to abandon *all*—or "the world" as Olcott then knew and described it—and wholly surrender oneself to the resulting adversities of probation and beginning chelaship under one of the Adepts. But Olcott's experience is actually *not* a useful paradigm applicable to most today who may be at the crossroads of making such a decision, followed immediately by such a commitment. Olcott's experience, while intriguing and inspiring to read, was at the same time a rare anomaly that would apply only to a minute percentage of those who may be, for various reasons, specially positioned to assist the Adepts in their missions. These missions are nearly always the same in terms of providing spiritual clarity and enlightenment to humanity consistent with their *bodhisattva* ideal, which was exactly what they then did in using and guiding HPB and Olcott as their agents "working in the world." This method they use because the Adepts, by their own repeated admissions in these and similar terms "rarely show any outward signs by which to be recognized or sensed."[5] The Adept Morya's visit to Olcott in New York was a clear but necessary exception to this normal practice of reclusivity.

To be honest, in the aftermath of such an experience as Olcott's, most spiritual wayfarers would likely consider it a relatively easy decision to reach the point of abandoning all and surrendering themselves full-time to the sacred work of the Adepts, being no less than the spiritual enlightenment of all humanity. Following any similar event, an indestructible conviction would no doubt strike such a wayfarer, as it did Olcott, with all the speed and power of a lightning bolt that would instantly cauterize any and all doubts they may have had.

The more difficult decision to make, however, and the decision faced by most such wayfarers today, is to "abandon all" in the *absence* of any such empirical confirmation of the Adepts' existence, their rules and methods, and their oversight of probationers and *chelas*. This is because their existence, and their sacred Order, have been effectively confirmed in the minds of many wayfarers due not only to numerous accounts of the extraordinary, and voluntary, multiple appearances of several of these Adepts in the last quarter of the nineteenth century, but also to the surviving written corpus of materials they sent as letters to their *chelas*. Olcott's great fortune was to have had all doubt dissolved in an instant by this overwhelming empirical and confirmatory experience of his own *guru's* visit, even though occult in nature. The final result for Olcott was the immediate manifestation of a steel conviction of the truth of the existence of the Adepts, and the fundamental purpose and methods of their mission.

In contrast to Olcott's experience, most spiritual wayfarers today who approach the precincts of probation must rely *exclusively* on their reason and intuition to make this momentous decision. They must excise doubts about the existence of the Adepts and their mission and replace them with an invincible conviction—this replacement, it should be emphasized, being based not on some aspirational "faith," but on evidence and the knowledge it supports. Once this decision is made,. and the wayfarer is thus in an interim state of free-fall, there must follow an exertion of will in "forcing circumstances to bow before you"[6] in advancing on this path to "come to us," in the Adept's words, as a probationer and *chela*.

The wonderful favor given to Olcott by his *guru* Morya was no doubt both well deserved and necessary for the mission at that moment, but it would be a mistake for those spiritual wayfarers now on the cusp of such a decision to imagine such an event occurring in their cases. Normally, further advancement on the higher spiritual path would require that one's reason and intuition be developed to a point where by them alone, in the absence of any extrinsic evidence or phenomena, the *same* steeled conviction as Olcott announced in his memoir is achieved by the wayfarer. But to overcome doubt and achieve conviction in this way is no easy feat, both in the past and especially now in the 21st century. However, there do exist resources today, evidentiary in nature, that were unavailable in the 1870s, and those resources should be useful to wayfarers who approach the gate through which they can pass, if qualified, and advance in earnest toward chelaship and initiation.

Even if among the true tests for being accepted as a *chela* of an Adept is achieving conviction in the absence of extrinsic evidence by reliance on a close collaboration of reason and intuition, it is fair to say that *some* doubt may continue to exist within the consciousness of a probationer until he or she reaches that point of complete conviction. Most of any wayfarer's doubts either about the impact of their decision on those in their lives, or about the Adepts—their extraordinary powers (*siddhis*), their hard rules and enigmatic methods, or the strategies used in their sacred mission—would need to be excised prior to entering probation. But as the normally seven-year period of probation is the proving ground for aspiring *chelas*, some stubborn doubts harbored deep within may remain a challenge for the wayfarer during this time. Moreover, such stubborn doubts may even be employed and stoked by the *guru* as the blacksmith stokes his furnace using, perhaps somewhat surprisingly, the method of deception. Deception can both inflame existing doubts and create new ones in the mind of the probationer, if he or she lacks sufficient discrimination and intuition to detect deception.

Deception is an efficient method unapologetically affirmed by Adepts for training and testing prospective *chelas*. As KH asserted, "A chela under probation is allowed to think and do whatever he likes. He is warned and told beforehand: 'You will be tempted and deceived by appearances...'"[7] But KH and Morya were also both acutely aware that to the European gentleman or lady of the late-nineteenth century, if not to the Western mind generally, deception—the willful act of deceiving another—was considered an offense of some magnitude. More than one letter in the correspondence of these two Adepts to their Western *chelas* contained some discourse on this principle. What these Adepts sought to convey to these *chelas* were the high stakes involved in the training they would be undertaking, and especially in the use of will where doubt may exist—doubts often being the progeny of deception. Only the ability, or skill, of being able to unmask deception and deceit and see the underlying truth by a prospective *chela* would allow him or her to proceed safely to the next level of training, to develop the will of commission and, perhaps, even certain occult powers. "[W]e work and toil," concludes KH, "and allow our chelas *to be temporarily deceived*, to afford them means never to be deceived hereafter, and to see the whole evil of falsity and untruth, not alone in this but in many of their after lives."[8]

If the probationer is able to be deceived, and having been deceived such deception leads to doubt regarding one's spiritual path forward, as it often does, then this ability to be deceived is in fact a disability as it pertains to progress on that path. This is because doubt, which can also be defined as the antithesis of conviction, is unarguably a hindrance and often an obstacle to occult training and ascending higher on the spiritual path. KH, without mincing words, advised one of his *chelas* this way: "Take care Mohini Mohun Chatterjee—doubt is a dangerous cancer."[9] We also learn from them, significantly, that doubt is a common problem for probationers: "Why is it that doubts and foul suspicions seem to beset every aspirant for chelaship?"[10]

The resolution to defeating these "doubts and foul suspicions" is simpler than it may appear. It is resolved by adhering to the wise counsel of the Adept Tuitit Bey: "TRY. Rest thy mind—banish all foul doubt."[11] The resting of one's mind in meditation invariably arrests the furious scramble of doubts that plague the anxious wayfarer, and opens the way to conviction. So, it is only by *trying* in this effort, and if at first the wayfarer fails, by trying again, *etc.*, that doubts preventing his or her advancement will ultimately be banished from the psyche, and a decision to "abandon all" can at last be made. Trying is never a guarantee of success, but success will never be achieved without first trying. This momentous decision, once engaged, can also amplify conviction, which similarly aligns with the concluding advice of Tuitit Bey to "open thy Spirit to conviction." Proportionally, as doubt is banished conviction increases, and greater conviction leads the wayfarer to the strength needed to decide to *"abandon all* and come to us."

There has been no time either in the relatively short span of "recorded history" or in the later rounds and lesser cycles of the spiritual evolution of humanity on Earth, as carefully outlined in Volume II of HPB's *The Secret Doctrine*, in which the Adepts of the spiritual hierarchy of humanity did not receive, according to their tradition, aspiring neophytes as new probationers and *chelas* for training and advancement toward Adeptship. At special zeniths of these cycles, representing both the end of a past and beginning of a future cycle, extraordinary efforts have been made by these Adepts to promulgate the ancient wisdom to a wider segment of humankind. One such effort, during the last quarter of the nineteenth century, was the publication in modern English of immemorial spiritual truths and principles through the pen of HPB and others in her immediate orbit. Closely allied to the publication of these materials were extraordinary multiple appearances to prospective *chelas* and close associates by several of these Adepts during this time. But even more significantly, for the first time in recorded history such Adepts have left to posterity *their own* writings in the form of hundreds of personal handwritten letters to dozens of *chelas*. Beginning in the early 1920s, many of these letters became available to the public through publication, which provided a wealth of facts and details not only about the doctrine and sacred philosophy of the Adepts, but also about the existence, rules, methods, labors, and mission of this hieratic Order of Adepts.

Henry Olcott, as we have seen, was fortunate to have had direct contact with his *guru*, Morya, and as a prospective accepted *chela* with such direct contact, he was instantaneously and with little difficulty enabled to make his decision to abandon all and follow his *guru*. However, those wayfarers today who may be on the cusp of such a decision are also blessed in their own way, having the unprecedented benefit of access to a large corpus of materials written by several of these Adepts that provides in its pages a map to guide such wayfarers in the ways of chelaship and ascending the higher reaches of the spiritual path.[12] Since the publication of *Letters from the Masters of the Wisdom* (1st and 2nd Series) from 1919, and *The Mahatma Letters to A.P. Sinnett* in 1923, the world at large and the wayfarers in it have had an exceptional opportunity to realize and to accept the truth of their existence, which are both powerful antidotes to doubt.

None of the first fellows of The Theosophical Society in the 1870s and 1880s had access to any such published letters. With the exception of those like Olcott who had direct access to the Adepts, or very few others who had access to them through HPB, the majority of those fellows, it could be argued, were in that same category of wayfarers who needed to rely exclusively on reason and intuition to make the decision to abandon all and exert their will in following an Adept. Prior to 1875, knowledge of the Adepts and their Brother/sisterhood was typically acquired by traditional means, within the esoteric elements of contemplative religious orders or secret societies, and was not widely circulated. This process, however, underwent a change with the publication of the letters of these Adepts, and with the writings of HPB on chelaship and treading the higher spiritual path. This valuable body of esoteric writings allows today's wayfarers—wherever they may be—to have at their discretion an opportunity to read and familiarize themselves with these truths. The more expert the wayfarer becomes in the command of this literature, the fewer doubts he or she should have.

As a final thought to this discussion, the question of *self-doubt* must be addressed. Within this context, self-doubt may be described as an introversion of any larger, existing doubts that burden the wayfarer regarding the Adepts and their existence. Under these circumstances, self-doubt usually appears as a question of whether one is truly equipped to succeed on the higher spiritual path to become a *chela*—of whether one has the requisite courage, strength, selflessness, charity, and purity to succeed. But this specific issue is more a matter of inner self-confidence, than doubt about outer circumstances. And while self-doubt can be a hindrance on the spiritual path whose significance should by no means be minimized, it is only indirectly related to that level of conviction the wayfarer must achieve regarding the existence of the Adepts, their powers (*siddhis*), their hard rules and enigmatic methods, the strategies used in their mission of compassion, or the necessity of abandoning all and going to them. Within these circumstances, self-doubt also reaches to one's own fear of failure to achieve reaching or interacting with an Adept, after having made the hard and often irreversible decision to abandon all in order to do so. Nonetheless, such self-doubt must also be controlled, if not overcome entirely, before the wayfarer can meaningfully proceed.

Doubt in all its forms can be both a hindrance to and a danger upon the spiritual path. As KH observed, "Once fairly started on the way to the great Knowledge, to doubt is to risk insanity; to come to a dead stop is to fall; to recede is to tumble backward, headlong into an abyss."[13] While doubt may be the principal cause of failure or even insanity for those on probation or beginning chelaship, it may as easily incite the wayfarer's coming to a dead stop or receding along the path, as well. Yet if the wayfarer will but daily live a pure and spiritual life, and *try*, and keep trying, this is what he or she will discover: "Little by little your sight will clear, you will find the mists pass away, your interior faculties strengthen, your attraction towards us gain force, and certainty [conviction] replace doubts."[14] Then can the life-altering decision be made to "*abandon all* and come to us," without being diverted by trepidation, equivocation or crippling doubt.

11

Voice of the Silence: Whispers of the Intuition

Happy is he whose spiritual perceptions ever whisper truth to him!
– Koot Hoomi

The *Sāvitrī* (*Gāyatrī*) mantra is a revered verse from a *sukta* (an entire hymn) of the sacred scripture *Rigveda* (3.62.10), which dates to approximately 1500 BCE. When chanted properly with meter, the *Sāvitrī* mantra is quite beautiful and spiritually awesome. The mantra's brief invocation is directed to the solar deity, who is asked among other things to enlighten our "intuition" (or "minds" or "intellect" or "understanding"). The English language term employed depends on which of the various modern translations from the Sanskrit is consulted.

It hardly seems surprising that what we may term *intuition* was foremost in the minds of authors of the *Vedas* who, so long ago, first recorded the centrality of its function for spiritual development. But just as intuition has also been a key subject of esoteric teachings in the written record since Vedic times, it is more significantly a core value or principle of the immemorial *philosophia perennis* or perennial philosophy which, being also immutable, is neither subject to nor affected by time.

The English term intuition is rendered differently in different spiritual traditions. In ancient Greece it was referred to as *gnosis*, the study of which may be termed gnoseology. In Sufi sacred texts, the Arabic term used is *ma'rifa*. Hinduism contains references in Sanskrit to two separate terms for intuition, being *prajñā* and *jñāna*, both of which according to its sacred texts operate through the 6th principle of the human being, or *buddhi*. The term *buddhi*, to refresh our memory, appears in the Vedantic doctrine of the *kośas* or "subtle bodies"—alternatively "sheaths" or "vehicles" or "envelopes"—of which the *vijñānamaya-kośa* or *buddhi* is one. While not the substance of intuition, *buddhi* is properly the human modality through which the faculty of intuition operates as a process. HPB and her teachers used the English terms "intuition" or "intellectual intuition" to describe the same faculty as do the aforementioned terms, and correspondingly also described the *buddhi*. Instead of intuition, Ananda Coomaraswamy preferred the English term "intellection," as being the process or operation of the "spiritual intellect."

It should be noted, before leaving the subject of translation, that *prajñā* and *jñāna* are both often translated as intuition most likely because both *prajñā* and *jñāna* share the common Sanskrit root *jñā* ("to know"). Though these two terms signify different things, they are closely related and share a certain synonymy. In both the classic Hindu and theosophic doctrines, these dual "sides" of intuition are equally important for the wayfarer to understand and develop. The proper functioning of both is needed in order for the wayfarer to make any meaningful advancement on the higher spiritual path.

These foregoing and basic facts are enough to conclude that the intuition plays a central and crucial role in genuine spiritual development, and that this has always and everywhere been the case. Accordingly, for the wayfarer on the higher spiritual path, a deep and abiding focus on understanding and developing the intuition is a *sine qua non* for effective progress. No greater reason for the need of this focus exists than that reason of which HPB reminded us above: "And, remember, it is by the inner, not the outer, self that we come into relations with Adepts and their advanced Chelas." This coming "into relations with" the Adepts through our Inner Selves can only be wholly effected by means of the intuition.

Two main features among multiple features of the faculty of intuition highlighted by their Sanskrit renderings exist together in connection with the modality of the subtle intuitive principle (or *buddhi*). One of the two main features is that which allows the aspirant to unlock the meaning of sacred and profound esoteric principles of metaphysics, or *prajñā*, usually presented by either oral or scriptural means, including symbols. The other main feature, or *jñāna*, could be described as a form of reading signs or omens in action or events, or perhaps prescience, and also further though cautiously described as a form of communication. In this occult form of communication, *guru* and *chela* may, without words, actively and clearly receive and transmit psychic impressions metaphysically, once the *chela* becomes sufficiently equipped to participate in this way through advanced training.

Ultimately it does not matter which of these terms, in whatever language, we decide to use to describe the faculty and operation of intuition, as long as we are clear about what is being discussed and how it operates. In its most succinct formulation, intuition can be defined as the faculty whereby the perceiver is immediately able both to presciently grasp the core of active phenomena and receive/transmit psychic impressions, and to achieve or realize *direct* knowledge and understanding of first principles (truths), being universal sacred principles that are immemorial and immutable. Moreover, a further and equally significant component of this definition is the perceiver's deliberate choice to *apply* the directly perceived signs, impressions and knowledge to contingent circumstances— those of one's life, for example. All this involves a level of "suprarational" knowledge, or understanding, or wisdom, that is not communicable through words as a transfer of this knowledge, but is effectively *realized* by the perceiver through the faculty of intuition through a process more like a merger with this knowledge. As HPB noted, "The whole essence of truth *cannot be transmitted from mouth to ear.* Nor can any pen describe it, not even that of the recording Angel, unless man finds the answer in the sanctuary of his own heart, in the innermost depths of his divine intuitions."[1]

Those formidable individuals who have achieved the highest levels of initiation and to whom many refer as Adepts—and their advanced students or *chelas*—would necessarily have fully (or highly) developed use of the intuition. Those wayfarers who would seek to join their ranks by ascending directly upward to the summit of spiritual realization, but who currently stand at the lower slopes of that steep and forbidding mountain, are likely to have varying degrees of capability in the proficient use of intuition. These varying degrees of proficiency in the use of intuition among such aspirants can plausibly be explained by the effects of the operation of mediate causes, or *karma*, that trace back to their activities in previous existences.

Whatever the case may be, wayfarers or spiritual aspirants differ in this regard: some have existing skills in the use of intuition, while others lack equal skills but may yet proceed on the spiritual path owing to other necessary qualities. Aspirants in both these categories, however, can make substantial progress *only* where conscious and deliberate efforts are made to undertake a sustained program of further developing and understanding the operation of intuition.

At this point the reader is asked momentarily to "shift gears," and form a mental picture of the biceps muscle of the human arm. As an infant, the undeveloped biceps is unnoticeable due to being buried in soft fatty tissue, but as the child grows, so the biceps—as do all other muscles in the body—grows and develops normally as well. As a young adult, the biceps may have developed good muscle definition and be clearly distinguishable from other muscles on the arm and shoulder, depending upon the congenital constitution and athletic development of the individual. Now, the reader is asked to form a mental picture of an accomplished bodybuilder, who trains by lifting weights daily to enlarge the biceps, and all the body's other muscles, to compete in bodybuilding competitions. This athlete's biceps eventually become massive, and this by means of one basic form of exercise: *repetition* of lifting heavy weights. As it turns out, basic principles of developing the intuition do not differ significantly from those of developing the biceps, or any other muscle. The wayfarer must use his or her intuition consciously and repeatedly, exert heartily, and then *rely* on the outcome of that use. In the beginning of this intuition training regime, errors in perceptions will undoubtedly occur. But over time, as the strength of the intuition grows, so will its accuracy and dependability. And repeated enough, the use of the intuition can finally develop as second nature, as it were, and the aspirant may advance, provided he or she remains true to the unyielding rules of the higher spiritual path and has the requisite courage and other necessary qualities.

It is evident to those who tread or seek to tread the higher spiritual path that among its inexorable outcomes, or goals, is to understand or gain direct knowledge (*prajñā*) of the esoteric first principles of metaphysics that form the basis of the *philosophia perennis*. This ability differs from but is closely related to the ability of the wayfarer to recognize *correspondences* of these principles in his or her spiritually directed activities, and even in all contingent circumstances, by means of the intuition. It is about intuition-as-*prajñā* that KH, referring to HPB's work *Isis Unveiled*, stated that "'Isis' was *not* unveiled, but rents sufficiently large were made to afford flitting glances to be completed by the student's own intuition."[2] Study is certainly part of the higher spiritual path, and while the mind (*manas*) may not be able to grasp how and what the intuition can, the harvest of the intuition may illumine those areas of the mind's comprehension that are able to be so illumined in order that it may have a more complete or holistic understanding of truth. The mind and the intuition almost always cooperate when both are fully active.

Works such as *The Secret Doctrine* and *The Voice of the Silence* by HPB were provided to us as maps to navigate the more enigmatic terrain of the spiritual path. These works are the more recent of the textual and scriptural restatements of the perennial philosophy, of *theosophia*, bequeathed to us by the great initiates of the past, too numerous to list here. To study and familiarize ourselves with these works is but one of the requirements of treading the higher spiritual path. And we can truly only unlock the deeper meanings contained in these works by use of intuition-as-*prajñā*, since their authors typically expressed themselves in such a way that by this faculty alone the "veiled" esoteric principles could be realized or "unveiled" by the student. A major objective of this intuition is to know directly the omniscient providential knowledge (pure wisdom) lying beyond contraries in the manifest and physical world of duality. This ability could also be described as being fully and constantly mindful—aware and conscious—in the *now*.

As explained by KH, "On close observation, you will find that it was never the intention of the occultists really to conceal what they had been writing from the earnest determined students, but rather to lock up their information for safety sake, in a secure safe-box, the key to which is—intuition."[3] These "secure safe-boxes" often take the form of parables and allegories within the written texts of such works, not unlike the classical "myths" occasionally found imbedded in the otherwise rational dialogues of Plato. HPB, while addressing this subject, noted that "It may be a parable and an allegory *within an allegory*. Its solution is left to the intuition of the student, if he only reads that which follows with his *spiritual eye*."[4] And without this ability to read or listen with the "spiritual eye" or intuition, and instead relying on the mind alone, the predictable outcome, as KH noted, would be that "... knowledge can only be communicated gradually; and some of the highest secrets—if actually formulated even in your well prepared ear—might sound to you as insane gibberish..."[5]

As critical as developing the intuition may be to the wayfarer, he or she should not succumb to the notion that reason and knowledge of the mind are unimportant in contrast to the intuition. Well developed human faculties—all of them—are necessary to reach the higher levels along the spiritual path, including a rational and bright mind. What is clear, however, is that the wayfarer should never confuse the two, or seek to rely solely on reason where the need is to rely on the intuition. A.P. Sinnett, it appears, may have been guilty of this, and so received an unapologetic observation from his Adept correspondent KH, who told him: "Unfortunately, however great your purely human intellect, your spiritual intuitions are dim and hazy, having been never developed."[6] Intuition-as-*prajñā*, therefore, could be fairly described as that suprarational faculty which is of greater utility for advancement on the spiritual path than the "purely" intellectual achievements of the wayfarer. As HPB pointed out, "Only those who realise how far Intuition soars above the tardy processes of ratiocinative thought can form the faintest conception of that absolute wisdom which transcends the ideas of time and space."[7] One can profitably compare this statement of HPB to one made by Albert Einstein in *Essays in Science*: "The supreme task of the physicist is to arrive at those universal elementary laws from which the cosmos can be built up by pure deduction. There is no logical path to these laws; only intuition, resting on sympathetic understanding of experience, can reach them."[8]

In light of the foregoing, there can be no doubt that the wayfarer must seek to develop intuition-as-*prajñā*, that element of intuition needed to penetrate subtle esoteric and cosmogonic principles of the universe such as those expressed, for example, in Book I, Part I of Volume I of *The Secret Doctrine*. But at the same time, the wayfarer should also undertake to develop that element of intuition that may be applied to the practical requirements of treading the spiritual path, referred to as *jñāna*. This corresponding side of the faculty of intuition, and its degree of usefulness, was addressed by KH: "Chelaship admits none of these [emotional-mental] transitions; its prime and constant qualification is a calm, even, contemplative state of mind (not the mediumistic passivity) fitted to receive psychic impressions from without, and to transmit one's own from within."[9]

An example from history perfectly illustrates this point. In 1884, C.W. Leadbeater sought affirmatively to become a *chela* of KH, and in so doing made a considered but uncharacteristically quick decision to depart England for India to pursue his goal and his training. In the wake of that intuitive decision, Leadbeater received a letter by occult means from his *guru*, who told him that "Since your intuition led you in the right direction and made you understand that it was *my desire* you should go to Adyar *immediately*, I may say more."[10] Leadbeater was in that moment, to use his *guru's* words, "fitted to receive psychic impressions from without," and it appears that he did.

The "psychic impressions" or "spiritual perceptions" to which KH referred, and that are "received" or realized or simply understood by the wayfarer's intuition-as-*jñāna*, come through a multiplicity of ways. Most of these ways are subtle, and are therefore aptly referred to as "whispers" of the intuition or, as stated in *The Voice of the Silence*, the "soundless sound." In the past century, modern psychology has developed excellent working models of nonverbal communication based on "body language" and facial micro-expressions, by which a trained psychologist can fairly accurately "read" the reactions of individuals to a variety of pressing issues and situations. But while this form of communication may be nonverbal, it is still physical. Conversely, the intuition, as *jñāna*, is able to perceive nonverbal and nonphysical impressions that provide a clear vision or comprehension of various situations faced by the wayfarer in his or her daily activities.

Those with well developed intuitions may hear through their Inner Person the whispers of the intuition, and this "hearing" may also occur through correctly reading signs, signals, clues, hints, and omens from a variety of different sources. When such individuals receive or realize truths as intuitional perceptions, they then *rely* on these perceptions which often affect key decisions and efforts that must be made on the higher spiritual path. It does one little good to have a well developed intuition if one ignores its perceptions. For these reasons KH, in counseling his *chela* Laura Holloway, stressed the importance for her to "Learn, child, *to catch a hint through whatever agency it may be given*" (emphasis in original).[11]

One can therefore see that the importance of developing intuition-as-*jñāna* is not just to make one's way safely through the vicissitudes of daily life, but also to create a necessary tool for advancement upon the higher spiritual path. And, for the wayfarer who aspires to align himself or herself with a *guru*, the need to develop the intuition aligns with becoming "... fitted to receive psychic impressions from without, and to transmit one's own from within." In this way will the *chela* and *guru* find the common ground for even greater advancement for the *chela*, since efficient expenditure of energy (and time) is a well known rule under which these *gurus* operate. For this reason, the exhortation of Serapis Bey to Henry Olcott to "Use your intuition, your innate powers, *try*, you will succeed...,"[12] was so often repeated by these Adepts to aspiring *chelas*. Trying, in this regard, is not unlike the commitment of a bodybuilder who strains each day to enlarge the biceps muscle to a competition level. The wayfarer must practice constant and committed repetition of use, extraordinary exertion, including, *e.g.*, regular *vipassanā* meditation, and reliance upon the insights and perceptions received to properly develop the intuition and thus gain insight.

Omitted so far from our discussion is mention of the prospect of immediate development of the faculty of intuition by means of full and permanent activation of the 6th primary or *ājñā chakra*, associated by correspondence with the *buddhi*, and sometimes referred to in the vernacular as the "third eye." This omission is purposeful because, if it is true that the probability of such an immediate development of this subtle plexus occurring for most spiritual aspirants is virtually *nil*, the harboring of any such hope by the aspirant for this to occur becomes a useless distraction, if not a digression from the path. In fact, even if such a full and immediate development were possible, it is almost a *non sequitur* that a faculty as central to the spiritual development of an aspirant as intuition would be delayed to some time after the beginning of his or her ascent to the summit of spiritual realization. This must necessarily be the case because, first, meaningful progress on the path requires *from the outset* reliance on a suitably developing intuition. And, second, each hierarchical level of spiritual reality or enumerated initiatic "degrees" is said to correlate directly to one of the primary *chakras* (and thus to their corresponding powers or *siddhis*) of the initiate. Therefore, this correspondence between full development of an initiate's latent 6th-principle faculty of intuition, and a correspondingly high degree of initiation, mandates that an immediate and permanent development of a hitherto undeveloped intuition would rarely, if ever, occur.

Far better that the wayfarer apply the model of the bodybuilder and enlarge his or her intuition by rigorously exercising it, while treading the higher spiritual path, by constant repetition of its use and reliance on its whispers that silently sound upon the inner ear. Together with daily meditation, this is the one sure and true method of advancement on the higher spiritual path. This is because for most, without assiduously using, working, and relying on the intuition, it will not develop. But when at last it does develop fully—at some future time where the level of initiation achieved corresponds to the *buddhi*—upon that day a complete and unconditioned use of the intuition is achieved, and the initiate can confirm that "There is but one road to the Path; at its very end alone the 'Voice of the Silence' can be [fully] heard."[13] Until that time, though, the wayfarer's most expedient course of action is making daily and steady progress, and heeding the counsel of Serapis Bey: "Use your will power, and may the benediction of Truth and the Divine Presence of Him the Inscrutable be upon thee and help thee to open thy intuition."[14]

12

Death & Its Aftermath on the Higher Spiritual Path

True philosophers make dying their profession.

– Socrates (in *Phaedo*)

Praemonitus praemunitus ("forewarned is forearmed") is an adage from antiquity that applies as well to the metaphysical transition between death and rebirth, as to anything. This ancient adage, when combined with another integral to the core doctrine of the perennial philosophy—being *memento mori* ("remember that you shall die")—impels those wayfarers who tread the higher spiritual path to undertake a deep and serious study of this transition from death to rebirth while incarnate and competent, using the available tools at their disposal. Such a deep and serious study may be more accurately described both as a practical necessity for the wayfarer, and further as a virtual forearming or *preparation* for undertaking this journey through the *post-mortem* states when that time arrives. That point in time is simultaneously an exit from one's present *in*carnation, and an entrance into the states of being following one's "*ex*carnation."

The need for such preparation by the wayfarer is due to the consequences of navigating this entire *post-mortem* transition well, or of failing to do so, either of which can have an impact on one's future spiritual journey through subsequent incarnations. Among the "available tools" referred to are, at the least, a core treatise of the "Tibetan Book of the Dead" customarily called the *Bardo Thödol*, and the corresponding writings on death and the *post-mortem* states by the Adepts Morya and KH, and by HPB. This because *both* these doctrines or approaches to the *post-mortem* transition are predicated on a symbiosis of (i) karma, and (ii) periodicity. "The law of KARMA," wrote HPB, "is inextricably interwoven with that of Re-incarnation."[1]

The Tibetan sacred treatise called the *Bardo Thödol* (Tibetan *bar-do thos-grol chen-mo*), whose literal translation is "The Great Liberation through Hearing," was first entitled *The Tibetan Book of the Dead* in 1927 by W.Y. Evans-Wentz. Yet the *Bardo Thödol* is only one in a larger corpus of similar texts and treatises on the traditional Tibetan Buddhist practices of death and dying. In the 2005 English translation published under the auspices of the 14th Dalai Lama and titled *The Tibetan Book of the Dead, First Complete Translation*[2] (hereafter "TBD"), the Contents include *fourteen* chapters on Vajrayāna Buddhist texts that deal with practices and methods to be employed at the time of death or shortly thereafter. These texts focus primarily on attaining liberation from rebirth; failing that, they discuss attaining a propitious rebirth in a new body. The *Bardo Thödol* is but one among these fourteen chapters, *all* of which together comprise the "Tibetan Book of the Dead" in its totality.

Bardo is a Tibetan term meaning a "gap" or an "in-between," which the TBD translates as "intermediate state" within the context of the three *bardos* pertaining to (i) consciousness of a person occupying a living physical body, and three *bardos* pertaining to (ii) the *surviving* consciousness of a person no longer occupying a living body. Though the *Bardo Thödol* expressly makes mention of six *bardos*, of which the first three pertain to the corporeal life we live from birth to death, these incarnate *bardos* are only briefly mentioned in passing in the text. Nonetheless, this should not be construed to diminish the significance of these first three *bardos*, since they appear together as equal to the last three excarnate *bardos* in the companion text that appears in TBD as the "Root Verses of the Six Intermediate States." Only the last three excarnate *bardos* that pertain to dying and the *post-mortem* states are those that constitute the main subject of the *Bardo Thödol*. These last three *bardos* describe in detail the effects on one's consciousness at the moment of death, followed by the various after-death experiences of the deceased as he or she transitions through the *post-mortem* states until liberation from the wheel of death and rebirth is achieved, or until the next rebirth.

The three intermediate states or *bardos* that are the principal subject of the *Bardo Thödol* and pertain to dying and being excarnate in the *post-mortem* states are (1) *chi-kha'i bardo* or the moment of death, (2) *chos-nyid bardo* or experiencing Reality (through interaction with the 100 peaceful and wrathful deities), and (3) *srid-pa bardo* or experiencing the process of rebirth. The first or *chi-kha'i bardo* is said to cover the time from the cessation of breath to the end of "the time it takes to eat a meal," and is comprised of *two* separate opportunities for the decedent to recognize the "inner radiance" and so achieve liberation. The first of these opportunities refers to recognition by the deceased of the "inner radiance of the ground," which term is also translated as "luminosity" or "clear light," being an all-pervasive white light. According to the text, where the deceased recognizes it and *understands* that it is the essence of his or her own conscious awareness, he or she achieves liberation from the wheel of death and rebirth (*samsāra*) in that moment of recognition.

The second of these opportunities is recognition of the "inner radiance of the path," or "second inner radiance." According to the text, at the moment of death the deceased enters into a swoon state devoid of all exterior sensory input during the time in which the first inner radiance appears. If the opportunity to recognize the first inner radiance is missed, then after the vital energy and consciousness of the deceased leaves the body, he or she momentarily recovers from the swoon state, regains conscious awareness, and becomes lucid. In this instance of extraordinary lucidity, between the passing of the first inner radiance but before the "bewildering experiences related to past actions have arisen," *i.e.*, the advent of the 100 peaceful and wrathful deities of the second *bardo*, the deceased has another opportunity in this second inner radiance to attain liberation.

The second or *chos-nyid bardo* commences only after the deceased has failed to achieve liberation in the first *bardo*. The TBD refers to this *bardo* as that of "experiencing Reality," and during this phase "the bewildering apparitions, [which are the products] of past actions, emerge."[3] These apparitions—the 100 peaceful and wrathful deities—appear amid "sounds, lights and rays of light," often evoking highly emotional or passionate reactions in decedents. First to appear are the 48 peaceful deities, most in the form of the "five enlightened families," and each family also represents a "realm," of which there are six altogether. The last to appear are the 52 wrathful deities and, pursuant to the classic pattern of polarity, they appear as converse or opposite mirror images of the peaceful deities. For the decedent, the objective of these frightful confrontations is to avoid both *aversion* and *attraction*. In confronting these deities, the decedent must avoid these two contrary reactions and instead dispassionately recognize the opportunity for liberation being offered. But most important, the decedent must recognize that these "apparitions" are his or her *own* psychological projections from the surviving consciousness that arise as consequences of his or her past actions in the incarnation prior to death.

Finally, at the commencement of the third or *srid-pa bardo* the decedent has effectively become the transmigrant, since the process of dissolution of lower principles that death brings has placed the transmigrant in *its* (no longer his or her) unobstructed and genderless "mental body" or consciousness, as the text indicates. At this stage, the transmigrant is in the *bardo* of rebirth, where two goals confront it: the first or primary goal is to avoid rebirth by blocking all entrances to wombs leading to a new incarnation. Should it fail in achieving that goal, then the secondary goal is to select a womb that will provide a propitious rebirth. As to the first goal, the TBD's text provides various methods and techniques to block entrances to wombs. As to the goal of selecting a womb for rebirth, the text advises that the best family into which to be reborn is one "... where the mother and father are deeply devout." Here the transmigrant is exhorted to think: "[O]nce I have taken on a body which is blessed with the merit of being able to act on behalf of all sentient beings, I shall [dedicate myself to] acting on their behalf!"[4] With this invocation of the *bodhisattva* ideal which is central to Vajrayāna Buddhism, the *post-mortem* transition is concluded and the transmigrant is ready to re-enter corporeal existence through rebirth.

There is no single monograph in the corpus of esoteric writings by HPB or her teachers Morya and KH that deals exclusively with the transition from death to rebirth, and that would substantively correspond to the TBD. Nonetheless, for those inclined to undertake a deep and serious study of this transition, multiple references to this subject appear in their published letters and treatises. And when collected and compiled, these multiple references provide not only clarity to the journey of the transmigrant through the *post-mortem* states, but a meaningful basis upon which draw comparisons with the TBD. While it is not feasible to identify and describe in any detail here this sizeable compilation of references, it is important to identify two indispensable elements of the *post-mortem* transition contained in this compilation without which little clarity can be achieved.

The first of these elements is an acknowledgment of the seven "principles" of the human being, specifically including the composition of the three surviving principles that actually make the entire journey from death to rebirth. These composite surviving principles—being the 7th principle or *ātmā*, the 6th principle or *buddhi*, and the higher 5th principle or *manas arupa*—have been variously labeled in Western esoteric literature.

But one finds them most commonly referred to as either the "spiritual Monad" or "spiritual Ego," or as the "transmigrant," though all these terms refer to the same consolidated three principles noted above. In particular, in the *post-mortem* transition the intense interaction or "struggle" of the highest four subtle principles in the intermediate states—the 4th and 5th together, as against the 6th and 7th together—determines which of these duads prevails, which in turn determines the future course of this spiritual Monad/Ego.

The second of these two elements is a seminal paragraph written by KH which appears further below that encapsulates the essence of the *post-mortem* journey, or transition, and upon which the esoteric or theosophic perception of this subject is based. But as prefatory to KH's seminal paragraph, and regarding the seven principles without the cognizance of which the *post-mortem* transition cannot be clearly understood, a correspondingly comprehensive statement about them was made by Morya:

Thus the *body* of man is wedded to and remains for ever within the body of his planet; his individual *jivatma* life principle, that which is called in physiology *animal spirits* returns after death to its source—*Fohat*; his *linga shariram* will be drawn into *Akasa*; his *Kamarupa* will recommingle with the Universal *Sakti*—the Will-Force, or universal energy; his "animal soul" borrowed from the breath of *Universal Mind* will return to the Dhyan Chohans; his sixth principle— whether drawn into or ejected from the matrix of the Great Passive Principle—must remain in its own sphere—either as part of the crude material or as an individualized entity to be reborn in a higher world of causes. The seventh will carry it from the *Devachan* and follow the new *Ego* to its place of re-birth...[5]

Unpacking this statement, we must note that Moyra's compatriot KH refers to the higher "principles" of human beings that are described here consistent with the Vedantic formulation of constituent *kośas*, or "bodies," as found in the Taittiriya Upanishad, as we have already noted above. We reiterate that the word "principles" for the three higher *kośas* was the term of choice for HPB and the Adepts, rather than those of other translators such as "vehicle" or "sheath" or "envelope."

It is also useful to recall here that the Vedantic *kośas* of *ātmā-buddhi-manas* align exactly with the three higher principles of HPB, KH, and Morya, and these writers consistently follow the numerical order in their writings that the *ātmā*, *buddhi*, and *manas* are the 7th, 6th, and 5th principles. Similarly, the *mortal* or lower four of these seven principles, the "lower quaternary," do not as easily lend themselves to comparisons with either of the Vedantic concepts of *kośa*, described above, or to *śarīra*, also translated as "body," of which there are three. The exceptions to this are the *sthūla-sharīra*, the gross physical body, which is the first of the septenary principles, and the *linga-sharīra*, an ethereal counterpart of the physical body composed of *ākaśa* and the second of the septenary principles. The third of the principles, composed of *fohat* energy, is referred to as *jivatma* or "life principle" by HPB, KH, and Morya. The fourth lower principle is referred to as the *kama-rupa*, and is the center of desire, emotion, and volition.

It is equally useful to iterate that the unique 5th principle—*manas* or mind—unlike the others is bifurcated between the lower mind of ordinary thoughts, and the higher mind of abstract and/or spiritual thought. We further remind the reader that in esoteric literature these two lower and higher aspects of *manas*, often referred to as *manas rupa* and *manas arupa*, are separated by a pivotal divide known as the *antahkarana*. For our purposes, it is necessary to understand that for most during the *post-mortem* journey the *manas arupa*, the higher mind—or in any event the highest portions of it—"joins" the 6ᵗʰ and 7ᵗʰ principles of *buddhi* and *ātmā* and together these three form the spiritual Monad—the transmigrant—the immortal surviving element of the human being that reincarnates.

The following seminal paragraph written by KH, which encapsulates the essence of the Adepts' and HPB's views of the *post-mortem* journey, is a *precís* version of their expanded doctrine:

"Bardo" is the period between death and rebirth—and may last from a few years to a kalpa. It is divided into three sub-periods (1) when the *Ego* delivered of its mortal coil enters into *Kama-Loka* (the abode of Elementaries); (2) when it enters into its "Gestation State"; (3) when it is reborn in the *Rupa-Loka* of Devachan. Sub-period (1) may last from a few minutes to a *number* of years... Sub-period (2) is "very long," as you say, longer sometimes than you may even imagine, yet proportionate to the *Ego's* spiritual stamina; Sub-period (3) lasts in proportion to the good KARMA, after which the *monad* is again reincarnated.[6]

While this recitation does not align with the three *bardos* of the *Bardo Thödol* in notable ways, this doctrine does divide the *post-mortem* transition into three segments, as does the *Bardo Thödol*, which KH calls "sub-periods."[7]

Before proceeding to conclusory remarks on this subject of ultimate gravity, it is important to emphasize a fact that might be misconstrued by anyone who infers from the doctrines of death and dying either in the Tibetan sources or in those of the *philosophia perennis* that these doctrines are somehow applicable only to Tibetan Buddhists and esotericists. It is an anthropological norm that traditional cultures like that of 19ᵗʰ-century Tibet, whether their traditions are oral or literate, are typically self-referent. That is to say, their sacred writings and oral teachings are seldom designed to be universally applicable, or comparative, or to refer to other cultures, but instead are normally addressed exclusively to their own adherents and orthodoxies. The *Bardo Thödol* is a good example of this, even though its authors—one perhaps being Padmasambhava— would likely have acceded to the simple fact that people of non-Buddhist cultures in other countries also die, and probably thus would not confront in the *bardos* any Vajrayāna Buddhist icons they had never before seen. While the text of the TBD does not suggest to the reader, for the reasons just mentioned, that the deceased should substitute his or her own socio-religious simulacra for the 100 peaceful and wrathful Buddhist ones, it should not be surprising that scholars of Tibetan Buddhism, psychologists, and even a Tibetan Rinpoche have made this exact suggestion.

The Adepts and HPB, however, approached the *bardo* not from a traditional Tibetan Buddhist perspective but from a whole-earth or *universal* perspective in which all human beings make the *post-mortem* journey from death to rebirth following a basic process or pattern. Assuming that in this journey the decedent confronts and struggles with its own issues in a "state of chaotic dreams" and "illusions that have been created by ourselves" as HPB stated, the employment of non-Buddhist simulacra becomes a virtual necessity.

This conclusion is supported by the Tibetan scholar Robert Thurman, who wrote that the Buddhist simulacra of the *Bardo Thödol* "... could be used by non-Buddhist practitioners who seek to mobilize the Tibetan art of dying to prepare for their own between-transition, while deepening their sense of contact with the images and deities of their own religion."[8] The renown psychologist Carl Jung, who wrote a "Psychological Commentary" as a Foreword to the Evans-Wentz translation of *The Tibetan Book of the Dead*, observed that in regard to the *Bardo*

Thödol "... one is perfectly free, if one chooses, to substitute Christian symbols for the gods of the Chönyid *Bardo*."[9] And Sogyal Rinpoche, a Tibetan Lama and author of *The Tibetan Book of Living and Dying*, similarly commented that "... the deities can take on forms we are most familiar with in our lives. For example, for Christian practitioners, the deities might take the form of Christ or the Virgin Mary." He added this summary remark: "But in whatever form the deities appear, it is important to recognize that there is definitely no difference whatsoever in their fundamental nature."[10] Thus we also have a Tibetan Rinpoche who, in a sense, is universalizing the *Bardo Thödol*. Taken together these observations only further support the proposition that there is no multiplicity of choices regarding death and the afterlife based on varying religious dogmas, but that the events of dying, death, and transition through the *post-mortem* states to rebirth are events fundamentally common to us all as human beings, regardless of ethnicity, culture or creed, and are thus universal.

What we experience during our incarnate existence—the sum of our actions and choices—necessarily affects our excarnate experience in the *post-mortem* transition. In both the Tibetan *Bardo Thödol* and the later published theosophic doctrine, the decedent passes through a process or test of *facing itself*, facing the effects of its past actions and choices. In the *Bardo Thödol*, this is the confrontation of our own psychological projections in the form of peaceful and wrathful deities in the *chos-nyid bardo*. In the theosophic system, this is the confrontation of which KH speaks when describing "... a 'death' struggle between the Upper [6th and 7th principles] and Lower [4th and 5th principles] dualities. If the upper wins, the sixth, having attracted itself the quintessence of *Good* from the fifth... follows its divine *elder* (the 7th) into the 'Gestation' State; and the fifth and fourth remain in association as an empty *shell*..."[11] The outcomes of these confrontations are never certain, and each differs. For this compelling reason the wayfarer treading the higher spiritual path, like the "true philosopher" of Socrates, should not fail to incorporate as an integral part of his or her *pre-mortem* daily yoga, a deep study of the art of dying and of seamlessly transitioning the *post-mortem* states utilizing these or similar practices:

- *A daily planting of germs or seeds in our pre-mortem consciousness that will assist in the post-mortem experience.* First, in this regard, KH wrote that a decedent must have enough "spiritual spoil" within the *manas* to enter *devachan*—the third "sub-period"—because if "... the spiritual spoil from the fifth will prove too weak to be reborn in Devachan... it will there and then re-clothe itself in a new body..."[12] Therefore, if a probationer or aspiring *chela* includes in his or her daily meditation a visual image of the *guru*, or commits to memory the initiatic rules in *Light on the Path* by Mabel Collins, *etc.*, in any time spent in *devachan* such an individual would necessarily recall these and other similar thoroughly ingrained images or texts there. Second, as to any spiritual milestone or achievement carried into the subsequent incarnation, Morya wrote that "Man has his seven principles, the germs of which he brings with him at his birth."[13] Therefore, the more *conscious* and affirmative planting of truly spiritual "germs" or seeds the wayfarer effects in his or her current incarnation, the more likely these will reappear in *devachan* and/or in subsequent incarnations.

- *The effect of one's thoughts at the moment of death, and thus the need for sustained mindfulness of the possibility of one's death at any time, being "memento mori."* KH wrote that at the moment of death, "That impression and thought which was the strongest naturally becomes the most vivid and survives so to say all the rest which now vanish and disappear forever, to reappear but in Devachan." He then adds, in the same vein, that "... we create ourselves our *devachan* as our *avitchi* while yet on earth, and mostly during the latter days and even moments of our intellectual, sentient lives."[14] Therefore, at the moment of death, either to be unmindful or to be in a mental state of panic or anger or self-pity, is to cast that shadow over both one's transition through the *post-mortem* states and to some degree even over one's next incarnation. However, when the moment of death is foreseeable and even precisely foreseen, greeting death with calm awareness and spiritual grace is to cast a sacred light over what lies ahead, and can only benefit the wayfarer's further progress. The greatest test, of course, is to maintain this calm awareness and spiritual grace in the face of a violent and/or painful death, through an affirmative willing to center one's consciousness within the Higher Self and calling upon every bit of the reserve of one's strength and courage.

• *Adapting the Tibetan practice of "p'howa" as a universally applicable esoteric system of practicing the art of death and dying.* The TBD's chapter on *Consciousness Transference: Natural Liberation through Recollection*[15] explains the practice known widely in Vajrayāna Buddhism as *p'howa*. The objective of *p'howa* is consciousness transference immediately prior to the moment of death, into one of the *kaya* states[16] of Buddha consciousness, effecting liberation from the wheel of death and rebirth. This text on consciousness transference in the TBD encourages regular practice and training in *p'howa* during one's incarnate life, from birth to death. The training is technical, and includes methods that bear close similarities to the yogic practices of *prānāyāma*, or the control and regulation of the breath, and *kundalinī* yoga, pertaining to the activation and control of the primary plexuses or *chakras* associated with the *nādīs* or channels of subtle energy within the physical body.

- *Recognition of correspondences between one's daily meditation and one's dream states, and the "death struggle" of the four higher principles in kama-loka.* Preparation to confront oneself and one's own psychological projections in this *post-mortem* death struggle can first be undertaken in one's daily meditation. This correspondence with the *post-mortem* states is through the wayfarer's mental focus on stilling the lower principles (Lower Self/Outer Person), and centering the consciousness in the higher principles (Higher Self/Inner Person), and thereby achieving a deeper meditative state. Both these tensions correspondingly reflect the classic death struggle of spirituality illustrated in pre-modern artistic depictions of St. George and the Dragon, in which the Saint (Inner Self) slays the Dragon (Outer Self). The wayfarer whose daily meditations include such recognition, even for a moment, will have anticipated the death struggle between the 4th/5th and the 6th/7th principles of which KH speaks that occurs in the *post-mortem* states. Similarly, the wayfarer may wish to recall and scrutinize his or her nightly dream events, and the interplay between "sweet" dreams corresponding to the peaceful deities of the *Bardo Thödol*, and nightmares corresponding to the wrathful deities, these too being yet another correspondence to and preparation for this *post-mortem* "death struggle" of the four highest principles.

It is not an overstatement to assert that practice of the art of dying and death, of *memento mori*, is but one of multiple methods of *yoga* ("union"). For the ordinary person, such a practice is invaluable; for the wayfarer treading the higher spiritual path, it is indispensable. There do exist other more thaumaturgic approaches to dying and death: that of a Tibetan *tchang-chub*, for example, described by KH as "... an adept who has... become exempt from the curse of UNCONSCIOUS transmigration... [and] instead of reincarnating himself only after bodily death..."[17] can transfer his consciousness into another or different body at any time, repeatedly if necessary. But such methods must be left to the highest initiates. What is of greatest importance for most wayfarers ascending the higher spiritual path is "to learn to die *before* you die," and so prepare oneself for a *post-mortem* process whose successful navigation will necessarily affect the direction of one's continued initiatic journey. The immediate culmination of this journey is to "abandon all and come to *us*," being the Adepts, so that after acceptance as a *chela* and initiation into that Order of which they are sworn members, one might thereafter achieve liberation from the wheel of death and rebirth and take one's place in the long line of *bodhisattvas* who exist only to serve and ultimately enlighten all of humanity.

Endnotes

• Mountain and Summit as the Path and Its Goal

1. Blavatsky, *The Secret Doctrine*, Vol. I, p. 127.
2. Aquinas, *Summa Theologiae*, p. 128.
3. Besant, *The Path of Discipleship*, paragraph 63.
4. Jinarajadasa, *Letters from the Masters of the Wisdom*, 1st Series, p. 70.
5. Chin, Jr., *The Mahatma Letters to A.P. Sinnett*, p. 73.
6. Jinarajadasa, *Letters from the Masters of the Wisdom*, 2nd Series, p. 46.

• Purification and the Higher Spiritual Path

1. Jinarajadasa, *Letters from the Masters of the Wisdom*, 2nd Series, p. 118.
2. *H.P. Blavatsky Collected Writings*, Vol. III, p. 265.
3. Chin, Jr., *The Mahatma Letters to A.P. Sinnett*, p. 73.
4. *Ibid.*, p. 299.
5. Jinarajadasa, *Letters from the Masters of the Wisdom*, 1st Series, p. 74.
6. Chin, Jr., *The Mahatma Letters to A.P. Sinnett*, p. 35.
7. *Ibid.*, p. 93.
8. *Ibid.*, p. 203.
9. *H.P. Blavatsky Collected Writings*, Vol. V, p. 291.
10. Chin, Jr., *The Mahatma Letters to A.P. Sinnett*, p. 138.
11. *Ibid.*, p. 8.
12. *H.P. Blavatsky Collected Writings*, Vol. IV, pp. 607-08.
13. Chin, Jr., *The Mahatma Letters to A.P. Sinnett*, p. 73.
14. *Ibid.*, p. 442.
15. *Ibid.*, p. 299.
16. *Ibid.*, p. 73.
17. *Ibid.*, p. 143.

18. Jinarajadasa, *Letters from the Masters of the Wisdom*, 1st Series, p. 28.

19. Chin, Jr., *The Mahatma Letters to A.P. Sinnett*, p. 68.

• **Reincarnation and the Higher Spiritual Path**

1. *H.P. Blavatsky Collected Writings*, Vol. 6, p. 239.

2. Chin, Jr., *The Mahatma Letters to A.P. Sinnett*, p. 120.

3. Blavatsky, *The Key to Theosophy*, p. 93.

4. Chin, Jr., *The Mahatma Letters to A.P. Sinnett*, p. 217.

5. Blavatsky, *The Secret Doctrine*, Vol. I, p. 232 fn.

6. Blavatsky, *The Secret Doctrine Dialogues: H.P. Blavatsky Talks with Students*, p. 592.

7. Blavatsky, *The Key to Theosophy*, p. 175.

8. Chin, Jr., *The Mahatma Letters to A.P. Sinnett*, p. 375.

9. Blavatsky, *The Voice of the Silence*, pp. 219-220.

10. Blavatsky, *The Secret Doctrine*, Vol. I, p. 119.

11. *H.P. Blavatsky Collected Writings*, Vol. 7, p. 51.

12. *Ibid.*, p. 52.

13. Chin, Jr., *The Mahatma Letters to A.P. Sinnett*, p. 193.

14. *H.P. Blavatsky Collected Writings*, Vol. 6, p. 328.

15. Chin, Jr., *The Mahatma Letters to A.P. Sinnett*, p. 209.

16. *Ibid.*, p. 263.

17. *H.P. Blavatsky Collected Writings*, Vol. 6, p. 241.

18. Blavatsky, *The Voice of the Silence*, pp. 251-52.

• **Karma and the Higher Spiritual Path**

1. Jinarajadasa, *Letters from the Masters of the Wisdom*, 1st Series, p. 70.

2. Chin, Jr., *The Mahatma Letters to A.P. Sinnett*, p. 190.

3. *Ibid.*, p. 114.

4. Blavatsky, *The Key to Theosophy*, p. 205.

5. Blavatsky, *Theosophical Glossary*, p. 173.

6. Chin, Jr., *The Mahatma Letters to A.P. Sinnett*, p. 198.

7. Blavatsky, *The Secret Doctrine*, Vol. II, p. 302.

8. Coomaraswamy, *Buddha and the Gospel of Buddhism*, p. 107.
9. Blavatsky, *Theosophical Glossary*, p. 173.
10. *H.P. Blavatsky Collected Writings*, Vol. 11, p. 144.
11. Blavatsky, *The Secret Doctrine*, Vol. II, p. 303.
12. *H.P. Blavatsky Collected Writings*, Vol. 10, p. 288.
13. Chin, Jr., *The Mahatma Letters to A.P. Sinnett*, p. 123.
14. *H.P. Blavatsky Collected Writings*, Vol. 7, p. 180 fn.
15. *Ibid.*, Vol. 12, p. 385.
16. Chin, Jr., *The Mahatma Letters to A.P. Sinnett*, p. 437.
17. Coomaraswamy, *Selected Papers: Metaphysics*, p. 403.
18. Blavatsky, *The Secret Doctrine*, Vol. II, p. 306.
19. Coomaraswamy, *Selected Papers: Metaphysics*, p. 368.
20. Blavatsky, *Theosophical Glossary*, p. 97.
21. Jinarajadasa, *Letters from the Masters of the Wisdom*, 1st Series, p. 8.

• Consciousness and the Higher Spiritual Path

1. Blavatsky, *The Secret Doctrine*, Vol. I, p. 272.
2. Chin, Jr., *The Mahatma Letters to A.P. Sinnett*, p. 182.
3. Blavatsky, *The Secret Doctrine*, Vol. I, p. 199.
4. *Ibid.*, p. 200.
5. *H.P. Blavatsky Collected Writings*, Vol. 12, p. 532.
6. Chin, Jr., *The Mahatma Letters to A.P. Sinnett*, p. 273.
7. Blavatsky, *The Secret Doctrine*, Vol. I, p. 296.
8. *H.P. Blavatsky Collected Writings*, Vol. 11, p. 451.
9. Blavatsky, *The Key to Theosophy*, p. 121.
10. *H.P. Blavatsky Collected Writings*, Vol. 8, pp. 339-40.
11. Blavatsky, *The Key to Theosophy*, pp. 178-79.
12. *H.P. Blavatsky Collected Writings*, Vol. 11, p. 451.
13. *Ibid.*, Vol. 8, p. 96.
14. Chin, Jr., *The Mahatma Letters to A.P. Sinnett*, p. 73.
15. *Ibid.*, pp. 275-76.
16. Bhikkhu Bodhi, *In the Buddha's Words*, p. 240.
17. Chin, Jr., *The Mahatma Letters to A.P. Sinnett*, p. 376.

18. Blavatsky, *The Key to Theosophy*, p. 10.
19. *H.P. Blavatsky Collected Writings*, Vol. 12, p. 133.
20. Blavatsky, *The Secret Doctrine*, Vol. I, p. 166.
21. Chin, Jr., *The Mahatma Letters to A.P. Sinnett*, p. 75.
22. *Ibid.*, p. 210.
23. Blavatsky, *The Key to Theosophy*, p. 108.
24. Chin, Jr., *The Mahatma Letters to A.P. Sinnett*, p. 211.

- **Expanded Use of Will on the Higher Spiritual Path**

1. Jinarajadasa, *Letters from the Masters of the Wisdom*, 2nd Series, p. 102.
2. Blavatsky, *Theosophical Glossary*, p. 370.
3. Chin, Jr., *The Mahatma Letters to A.P. Sinnett*, p. 119.
4. *Ibid.*, Appendix II, p. 513.
5. *H.P. Blavatsky Collected Writings*, Vol. 4, p. 491.
6. Chin, Jr., *The Mahatma Letters to A.P. Sinnett*, p. 422.
7. Jinarajadasa, *Letters from the Masters of the Wisdom*, 2nd Series, p. 38.
8. Blavatsky, *Practical Occultism*, pp. 45-46.
9. *Ibid.*, pp. 50-51.
10. Blavatsky, *Theosophical Glossary*, p. 370.
11. Chin, Jr., *The Mahatma Letters to A.P. Sinnett*, p. 37.
12. *Ibid.*, p. 106.
13. Jinarajadasa, *Letters from the Masters of the Wisdom*, 1st Series, p. 123.
14. Chin, Jr., *The Mahatma Letters to A.P. Sinnett*, p. 59.
15. Blavatsky, *The Key to Theosophy*, p. 68.
16. *H.P. Blavatsky Collected Writings*, "Chelas and Lay Chelas," Vol. 4, p. 607.

- **Free Will in Light of the Higher Spiritual Path**

1. Blavatsky, *Theosophical Glossary*, p. 370.
2. Chin, Jr., *The Mahatma Letters to A.P. Sinnett*, p. 257.
3. Berkeley, CA: University of California Press, 2011.

4. Coomaraswamy, *Selected Papers: Metaphysics*, p. 91.
5. Coomaraswamy, *Selected Letters of Ananda K. Coomaraswamy*, p. 135.
6. Collins, *The Idyll of the White Lotus*, p. 141.
7. New York: Harper & Row, 1975. Eliade's many published works are replete with this theme. *See also*, Coomarasway's "*Ātmayajña*: Self-Sacrifice" (p. 107) and "The Meaning of Death" (p. 426) in *Selected Papers: Metaphysics*.
8. Brooks, "Free Will," unpaginated.
9. Coomaraswamy, *Selected Letters of Ananda K. Coomaraswamy*, p. 135.

• Love & Hatred on the Higher Spiritual Path

1. *See*, particularly, the tractate from the Gnostic scriptures titled "The Thunder, Perfect Mind": "For I am the first and the last, I am the honored one and the scorned one, I am the whore and the holy one," *etc.* From, Robinson, *The Nag Hammadi Library*, p. 271.
2. Blavatsky, *The Secret Doctrine*, Vol. II, p. 162.
3. Chin, Jr., *The Mahatma Letters to A.P. Sinnett*, p. 209.
4. *Ibid.*, p. 263.
5. *Ibid.*, p. 193.
6. *Ibid.*, p. 213.
7. *Ibid.*, p. 209.
8. *Ibid.*, p. 120.
9. *Ibid.*, p. 264.
10. *Ibid.*, p. 215.
11. *Ibid.*, p. 504.
12. *H.P. Blavatsky Collected Writings*, Vol. 14, p. 105.
13. Jinarajadasa, *Letters from the Masters of the Wisdom*, 2nd Series, p. 101.
14. Chin, Jr., *The Mahatma Letters to A.P. Sinnett*, p. 92.
15. Blavatsky, *The Voice of the Silence*, p. 208.
16. *H.P. Blavatsky Collected Writings*, Vol. 12, p. 434.

17. Chin, Jr., *The Mahatma Letters to A.P. Sinnett*, p. 100.

• The Providential Higher Spiritual Path
1. Williams, *Judaism*, p. 158.
2. Blavatsky, *Isis Unveiled*, Vol. II, p. 374.
3. *H.P. Blavatsky Collected Writings*, Vol. 6, p. 180.
4. *Ibid.*, p. 140.
5. *Ibid.*, Vol. 4, p. 501.
6. *Ibid.*, Vol. 6, p. 321.
7. Blavatsky, *The Secret Doctrine*, Vol. II, p. 305.
8. *Ibid.*, Vol. I, p. 643.
9. Chin, Jr., *The Mahatma Letters to A.P. Sinnett*, p. 198.
10. Jinarajadasa, *Letters from the Masters of the Wisdom*, 2nd Series, p. 35.
11. *H.P. Blavatsky Collected Writings*, Vol. 14, p. 396.
12. Chin, Jr., *The Mahatma Letters to A.P. Sinnett*, p. 473.
13. *Ibid.*, p. 294.
14. These *chelas*, Damodar and DK, were both veterans of the struggle to "leave home," and its costs. DK's nickname was "the disinherited" because he was disinherited by his family when he became a *chela* of KH. Damodar suffered a similar familial fate, for much the same reason.
15. Chin, Jr., *The Mahatma Letters to A.P. Sinnett*, p. 299.
16. Jinarajadasa, *Letters from the Masters of the Wisdom*, 1st Series, p. 75.
17. Chin, Jr., *The Mahatma Letters to A.P. Sinnett*, p. 73.
18. Caldwell, *Mrs. Holloway and the Mahatmas*, p. 123.
19. Jinarajadasa, *Letters from the Masters of the Wisdom*, 2nd Series, p. 11.

• Doubt & Conviction on the Higher Spiritual Path
1. Chin, Jr., *The Mahatma Letters to A.P. Sinnett*, p. 73.
2. Olcott, *Old Diary Leaves*, Vol. 1, p. 379.
3. *Ibid.*, p. 376.

4. *Ibid.*

5. Jinarajadasa, *Letters from the Masters of the Wisdom*, 1st Series, p. 74.

6. Jinarajadasa, *Letters from the Masters of the Wisdom*, 2nd Series, p. 69.

7. Chin, Jr., *The Mahatma Letters to A.P. Sinnett*, p. 222.

8. *Ibid.* A similar statement was made by Morya to E.W. Fern, who piously proclaimed high rank in an esoteric society he claimed would *never* condone deceit: "Well, this suspicion led me to think that one so high in a Society *that neither tolerates nor practices deceit*, could not care to belong to our poor Brotherhood *that does both*—regarding its probationists." Jinarajadasa, *Letters from the Masters of the Wisdom*, 2nd Series, p. 143.

9. Jinarajadasa, *Letters from the Masters of the Wisdom*, 1st Series, p. 42.

10. Chin, Jr., *The Mahatma Letters to A.P. Sinnett*, p. 451.

11. Jinarajadasa, *Letters from the Masters of the Wisdom*, 2nd Series, p. 11.

12. *See,* Quinn, *The Chela's Handbook*, being a selection of sentences and paragraphs drawn from the 19th-century letters of multiple Adepts pertaining specifically to the requirements of becoming—and remaining—a *chela* of an Adept.

13. Chin, Jr., *The Mahatma Letters to A.P. Sinnett*, p. 48.

14. Jinarajadasa, *Letters from the Masters of the Wisdom*, 1st Series, p. 74.

• Voice of the Silence: Whispers of the Intuition

1. Blavatsky, *The Secret Doctrine*, Vol. II, p. 516.

2. Chin, Jr., *The Mahatma Letters to A.P. Sinnett*, p. 121.

3. *Ibid.*, p. 279.

4. Blavatsky, *The Secret Doctrine*, Vol. II, p. 94.

5. Chin, Jr., *The Mahatma Letters to A.P. Sinnett*, p. 73.

6. *Ibid.*, p. 351.
7. Blavatsky, *The Secret Doctrine*, Vol. I, p. 2.
8. Einstein, *Essays in Science*, "Principles of Research," p. 4.
9. Jinarajadasa, *Letters from the Masters of the Wisdom*, 1st Series, p. 73.
10. *Ibid.*, p. 32.
11. *Ibid.*, p. 75.
12. Jinarajadasa, *Letters from the Masters of the Wisdom*, 2nd Series, p. 39.
13. Blavatsky, *The Voice of the Silence*, p. 134.
14. Jinarajadasa, *Letters from the Masters of the Wisdom*, 2nd Series, p. 37.

• **Death & Its Aftermath on the Higher Spiritual Path**

1. Blavatsky, *The Secret Doctrine*, Vol. II, p. 303.
2. Coleman, *The Tibetan Book of the Dead, First Complete Translation.*
3. *Ibid.*, p. 234.
4. *Ibid.*, p. 299.
5. Chin, Jr., *The Mahatma Letters to A.P. Sinnett*, p. 119.
6. *Ibid.*, p. 194.
7. For a fuller explanation of this doctrine, *see* Quinn, "The Transition from Death to Rebirth, Part II," in Georgiades, Erica, ed., "*Memento Mori* Studybook." Pescia, Italy: EuST, 2018, p. 35.
8. Thurman, *The Tibetan Book of the Dead*, p. 72.
9. Jung, "Psychological Commentary" in Evans-Wentz, *The Tibetan Book of the Dead*, p. 11.
10. Sogyal Rinpoche, *The Tibetan Book of Living and Dying*, p. 288.
11. Chin, Jr., *The Mahatma Letters to A.P. Sinnett*, p. 193.
12. *Ibid.*, p. 213.
13. *Ibid.*, p. 120.

14. *Ibid.*, p. 209.
15. Coleman, *The Tibetan Book of the Dead, First Complete Translation*, p. 199. *See*, particularly, the instructions set forth on pages 202-204.
16. These are *nirmānakāya*, *sambhogakāya*, and *dharmakāya*, all post-liberation states.
17. Chin, Jr., *The Mahatma Letters to A.P. Sinnett*, p. 75.

Bibliography

Aquinas, T. (1975) *Summa Theologiae*. II.2q.26, art.4. Cambridge: Cambridge University Press.

Besant, A. (2015) *The Path of Discipleship*. Second Edition. Adyar: Theosophical Publishing House.

Bhante H. Gunaratana. (2002) *Mindfulness in Plain English*. Boston: Wisdom Publications.

Bhikkhu Bodhi, ed. (2005) *In the Buddha's Words*. Boston: Wisdom Publications.

Blavatsky, H.P. (n.d.) *Isis Unveiled*, Vols. I & II, Facsimile edition. Point Loma, CA: Theosophical University Press. (Originally published in 1877, New York: J.W. Bouton.)

_____. (1889) *The Key to Theosophy*. London: Theosophical Publishing Co.

_____. (1972) *Practical Occultism*, 4th edition. Adyar: Theosophical Publishing House.

_____. (1947) *The Secret Doctrine*, Vols. I & II, Facsimile edition. Los Angeles: The Theosophy Company.

_____. (2014) *The Secret Doctrine Dialogues: H.P. Blavatsky Talks with Students*. Los Angeles: The Theosophy Company.

_____. (1892) *Theosophical Glossary*. London: Theosophical Publishing Co.

_____. (1964) *The Voice of the Silence*, 2nd edition. Adyar: Theosophical Publishing House.

Brooks, R.W. (n.d.) "Free Will." https://www.theosophy.world/encyclopedia/free-will (Internet site, unpaginated). Manila: TPH.

Caldwell, D.H., ed. (2012) *Mrs. Holloway and the Mahatmas*. (Internet): Blavatsky Study Center.

Chin, Jr., V.H., ed. (1993) *The Mahatma Letters to A.P. Sinnett*. Quezon City, Philippines: Theosophical Publishing House.

Coleman, G. and Thupten Jinpa, eds. (2005) *The Tibetan Book of the Dead, First Complete Translation*. New York: Penguin Books.

Collins, M. (1884) *The Idyll of the White Lotus*. London: Reeves and Turner.

_____. (1972) *Light on the Path*. London: Theosophical Publishing House.

Coomaraswamy, A.K. (1969) *Buddha and the Gospel of Buddhism*. Hyde Park, NY: University Books.

_____. (1988) *Selected Letters of Ananda K. Coomaraswamy*. A. Moore, Jr., ed. Delhi: Oxford University Press.

_____. (1977) *Selected Papers: Metaphysics*, Bollingen Series LXXXIX, R. Lipsey, ed. Princeton: Princeton University Press.

_____. (1977) *Selected Papers: Traditional Art and Symbolism*, Bollingen Series LXXXIX, R. Lipsey, ed. Princeton: Princeton University Press.

Dvivedī, M.N., trans. (1934) *The Yoga-Sūtras of Patañjali*. Adyar: Theosophical Publishing House.

Einstein, A. (2009) *Essays in Science*, Facsimile Reprint of 1934 Edition. Mineola, New York: Dover Publications.

Eliade, M. (1975) *Rites and Symbols of Initiation: The Mysteries of Birth and Rebirth*. New York: Harper & Row.

Endsley, M.R. and D.J. Garland, eds. (2000) *Situation Awareness Analysis and Measurement*. Mahwah, NJ: Lawrence Erlbaum Associates Publishers.

Frede, M. (2011) *A Free Will: Origins of the Notion in Ancient Thought*. Berkeley, CA: University of California Press.

Guénon, R. (2001) *Man and His Becoming According to the Vedānta*. Ghent, NY: Sophia Perennis.

H.P. Blavatsky Collected Writings (1975) Vols. I-XV. Adyar: Theosophical Publishing House.

Jinarajadasa, C., comp. (2011) *Letters from the Masters of the Wisdom*, 1st Series (7th Ed.). Adyar: Theosophical Publishing House.

_____. (2002) *Letters from the Masters of the Wisdom*, 2nd Series (4th Reprint). Adyar: Theosophical Publishing House.

Jung, C. "Psychological Commentary" in Evans-Wentz, W.Y., comp. & ed. (1960), *The Tibetan Book of the Dead*, 3rd edition. London: Oxford University Press.

Olcott, H.S. (1974) *Old Diary Leaves*, Vols. I-VI, 3rd printing. Adyar: Theosophical Publishing House.

Quinn, W.W., comp. (2020) *The Chela's Handbook*. San Antonio: Turning Stone Press.

_____, (as Anonymous). (2013) "Adepts, Yogis, and Masters in the Works of René Guénon" in *Sacred Web*, Volume 30.

Radhakrishnan, S. (2019) *The Principal Upanishads*, 32nd impression. Noida, India: HarperCollins.

Robinson, J.M., ed. (1977) *The Nag Hammadi Library*. San Francisco: Harper & Row.

Shantideva, trans. by Padmakara Translation Group. (2008) *The Way of the Bodhisattva*. Boston: Shambhala.

Sogyal Rinpoche. (2002) *The Tibetan Book of Living and Dying*, 20th anniversary edition. New York: HarperOne.

Thurman, R.A.F., trans. (1994) *The Tibetan Book of the Dead*. New York: Bantam Books.

Tolle, E. (1999) *The Power of Now*. Vancouver: Namaste Publishing.

Wallace, B.A., trans. (1998) *Natural Liberation: Padmasambhava's Teachings on the Six Bardos*. Boston: Wisdom Publications.

Williams, J.G. (1980) *Judaism*. Wheaton, IL: Quest Books.

O-BOOKS

SPIRITUALITY

O is a symbol of the world, of oneness and unity; this eye represents knowledge and insight. We publish titles on general spirituality and living a spiritual life. We aim to inform and help you on your own journey in this life.
If you have enjoyed this book, why not tell other readers by posting a review on your preferred book site?

Recent bestsellers from O-Books are:

Heart of Tantric Sex
Diana Richardson
Revealing Eastern secrets of deep love and intimacy to Western couples.
Paperback: 978-1-90381-637-0 ebook: 978-1-84694-637-0

Crystal Prescriptions
The A-Z guide to over 1,200 symptoms and their healing crystals
Judy Hall
The first in the popular series of eight books, this handy little guide is packed as tight as a pill-bottle with crystal remedies for ailments.
Paperback: 978-1-90504-740-6 ebook: 978-1-84694-629-5

Take Me To Truth
Undoing the Ego
Nouk Sanchez, Tomas Vieira
The best-selling step-by-step book on shedding the Ego, using the
teachings of *A Course In Miracles*.
Paperback: 978-1-84694-050-7 ebook: 978-1-84694-654-7

The 7 Myths about Love...Actually!
The Journey from your HEAD to the HEART of your SOUL
Mike George
Smashes all the myths about LOVE.
Paperback: 978-1-84694-288-4 ebook: 978-1-84694-682-0

The Holy Spirit's Interpretation of the New Testament
A Course in Understanding and Acceptance
Regina Dawn Akers
Following on from the strength of *A Course In Miracles*, NTI
teaches us how to experience the love and oneness of God.
Paperback: 978-1-84694-085-9 ebook: 978-1-78099-083-5

The Message of A Course In Miracles
A translation of the Text in plain language
Elizabeth A. Cronkhite
A translation of *A Course In Miracles* into plain, everyday
language for anyone seeking inner peace. The companion
volume, *Practicing A Course In Miracles*, offers practical lessons
and mentoring.
Paperback: 978-1-84694-319-5 ebook: 978-1-84694-642-4

Your Simple Path
Find Happiness in every step
Ian Tucker
A guide to helping us reconnect with what is really important in
our lives.
Paperback: 978-1-78279-349-6 ebook: 978-1-78279-348-9

365 Days of Wisdom
Daily Messages To Inspire You Through The Year
Dadi Janki
Daily messages which cool the mind, warm the heart and guide
you along your journey.
Paperback: 978-1-84694-863-3 ebook: 978-1-84694-864-0

Body of Wisdom
Women's Spiritual Power and How it Serves
Hilary Hart
Bringing together the dreams and experiences of women across
the world with today's most visionary spiritual teachers.
Paperback: 978-1-78099-696-7 ebook: 978-1-78099-695-0

Dying to Be Free
From Enforced Secrecy to Near Death to True Transformation
Hannah Robinson
After an unexpected accident and near-death experience, Hannah
Robinson found herself radically transforming her life, while a
remarkable new insight altered her relationship with her father, a
practising Catholic priest.
Paperback: 978-1-78535-254-6 ebook: 978-1-78535-255-3

The Ecology of the Soul
A Manual of Peace, Power and Personal Growth for Real People
in the Real World
Aidan Walker
Balance your own inner Ecology of the Soul to regain your
natural state of peace, power and wellbeing.
Paperback: 978-1-78279-850-7 ebook: 978-1-78279-849-1

Not I, Not other than I
The Life and Teachings of Russel Williams
Steve Taylor, Russel Williams
The miraculous life and inspiring teachings of one of the World's
greatest living Sages.
Paperback: 978-1-78279-729-6 ebook: 978-1-78279-728-9

On the Other Side of Love
A woman's unconventional journey towards wisdom
Muriel Maufroy
When life has lost all meaning, what do you do?
Paperback: 978-1-78535-281-2 ebook: 978-1-78535-282-9

Practicing A Course In Miracles
A translation of the Workbook in plain language, with
mentor's notes
Elizabeth A. Cronkhite
The practical second and third volumes of The Plain-Language
A Course In Miracles.
Paperback: 978-1-84694-403-1 ebook: 978-1-78099-072-9

Quantum Bliss

The Quantum Mechanics of Happiness, Abundance, and Health

George S. Mentz

Quantum Bliss is the breakthrough summary of success and spirituality secrets that customers have been waiting for.

Paperback: 978-1-78535-203-4 ebook: 978-1-78535-204-1

The Upside Down Mountain

Mags MacKean

A must-read for anyone weary of chasing success and happiness – one woman's inspirational journey swapping the uphill slog for the downhill slope.

Paperback: 978-1-78535-171-6 ebook: 978-1-78535-172-3

Your Personal Tuning Fork

The Endocrine System

Deborah Bates

Discover your body's health secret, the endocrine system, and 'twang' your way to sustainable health!

Paperback: 978-1-84694-503-8 ebook: 978-1-78099-697-4

Readers of ebooks can buy or view any of these bestsellers by clicking on the live link in the title. Most titles are published in paperback and as an ebook. Paperbacks are available in traditional bookshops. Both print and ebook formats are available online.

Find more titles and sign up to our readers' newsletter at http://www.johnhuntpublishing.com/mind-body-spirit

Follow us on Facebook at https://www.facebook.com/OBooks/ and Twitter at https://twitter.com/obooks